It's All about Learning

It's All about Learning

The Struggle in Choosing Traditional Public Education or Privatization

Jeff Swensson

ROWMAN & LITTLEFIELD
Lanham • Boulder • New York • London

Published by Rowman & Littlefield
An imprint of The Rowman & Littlefield Publishing Group, Inc.
4501 Forbes Boulevard, Suite 200, Lanham, Maryland 20706
www.rowman.com

86-90 Paul Street, London EC2A 4NE, United Kingdom

British Library Cataloguing in Publication Information Available

Library of Congress Cataloging-in-Publication Data

Names: Swensson, Jeff, author.
Title: It's all about learning : the struggle in choosing traditional public education or
    privatization / Jeff Swensson.
Other titles: It is all about learning
Description: Lanham, Maryland : Rowman & Littlefield, 2023. | Includes bibliographical
    references and index. | Summary: "It's All About Learning asserts that education
    in America is headed down one of two roads: traditional public education or
    privatization education. Wedded to free market theory, privatization education is the
    realization of adult-centric intentions. In contrast, traditional public education is the
    pursuit of student-centric intentions"—Provided by publisher.
Identifiers: LCCN 2022046323 (print) | LCCN 2022046324 (ebook) | ISBN
    9781475869392 (cloth) | ISBN 9781475869408 (paperback) | ISBN
    9781475869415 (epub)
Subjects: LCSH: Education and state—United States. | Privatization in education—
    United States. | Public schools—United States. | Private schools—United States.
Classification: LCC LC89 .S89 2023 (print) | LCC LC89 (ebook) | DDC 379.73—dc23/
    eng/20221123
LC record available at https://lccn.loc.gov/2022046323
LC ebook record available at https://lccn.loc.gov/2022046324

To my family

Contents

Contents

Acknowledgments

This book, like the K–16 career that influenced it, reflects the professionalism of countless colleagues whose creativity, intellect, humility, perseverance, and lived experiences taught me the value of instruction and learning environments that engage the capabilities of all students.

It is with gratitude that I acknowledge the transformative educators from Mariemont High School, Downers Grove South, Northwestern University, Walt Disney Magnet School, Washburne Middle School, Stanley Field Junior High, McKinley Junior High, Butler University, Decatur Junior High, Stonybrook Middle School, Raymond Park Middle School, the MSD of Warren Township, Carmel Clay Schools, and Ball State University. The colleagues with whom I have served are the bedrock upon which this manuscript is constructed.

To Lynn Lehman, John Ellis, and Michael Shaffer with whom I have collaborated on five previous books—I owe my thanks for their keen sense of excellence in our profession. I owe a tremendous debt to Tom Koerner, Carlie Wall, and Kira Hall at Rowman & Littlefield for supporting books about traditional public education and for their patience with an author who always wanted to say one more thing.

Prologue

Here's the choice: learning for all students in traditional US public education or free market theory in privatization education.

Who will choose the future of learning in America? Who will write the narrative for the history of the future of public education that best serves students and the democracy in which they live?

This book is a reckoning with the contemporary struggle over choice about learning in public education. The history of the future for teaching and learning throughout the United States depends on choice aligned with one of two major perspectives: traditional public education or privatization education.

The profound implications of this struggle dictate that this book does not predict a future of education cluttered with gadgets, technology, distance learning, or adult-centric intentions. The future of US students is too important to focus on "chasing rabbits."

Instead, this book examines the extent to which the history of the future of education is written to engage all students with either *how to think* or what to think.

The struggle over choice about learning discussed in the forthcoming chapters shares the *arbiters of choice* that summarize the intentions of the two major perspectives. The intentions of marketplace education benefit when friends of privatization erect barriers in the pathway for learning traveled by traditional US public education.

Proponents of traditional US public education and proponents of privatization education write vastly different narratives. This book examines both narratives, the consequences of each narrative, and the fundamental purpose for teaching and learning that each perspective offers as the future.

This book fulfills three purposes:

1. Provide a discussion in which public educators, parents/caregivers, state authorities, citizens, and others can sort through the details necessary

to understand the implications and consequences of the contemporary struggle over choice about learning.

2. Engage readers with the effect of each major perspective on students, learning, and democracy.

3. Establish a platform from which traditional public educators in the twenty-first century see the imperative for reflection and action that chooses student-centric intentions as the baseline for the history of the future of traditional public education.

These purposes invoke a reckoning with what is unseen and what is instrumental about the ongoing struggle in US education. These purposes illustrate the role that traditional public educators must play to sustain and advance learning for all US students.

Chapter 1

Toward the Purpose of US Public Education

EMAIL
To: Traditional Public Educators
Fr: The Teacher Down the Hall
Re: What Is the Purpose of Public Education?

Public educators, all of us, know that a multitude of grievances land on our doorstep. Many of these are unfounded, some constitute "get betters," and others represent the struggle over learning and purpose now underway.

Phrased here (in uncharacteristically civil language) is the grievance from which America's struggle originates: *What is the primary purpose of US public education?* Critics eagerly share a perspective that answers this question with choice that veers away from the path taken by traditional public education.

Immersed in day-to-day duties and challenges, and heavily engaged in a student-centric purpose already, public educators set aside their answer to this question for another day.

The gist of this email and the discussion that follows is that, for traditional public educators, another day has arrived.

The time to enter the struggle to choose the primary purpose of US public education is now. The narrative written for public education today is the history that directs its future.

In the chapter that lies ahead, the "prose" crucial to a future narrative is explored. *Intentions* are introduced as the arbiters of choice for two major perspectives: *traditional US public education* and *privatization education.*

Instrumental agency, which predefines what is socially valuable for each major perspective, puts proponents of both major perspectives in position to identify intentions as either *learnable moments* or *inconvenient lessons.*

The influence of history as the future narrative for the purpose of public education is discussed here. The *role of the public sector* throughout US history provides a window through which educators can consider the broader impact of educational choice.

The choices that public educators, all of us, make will place one perspective or the other at the center of the narrative for the history of the future of US public education.

DOES TRADITIONAL US PUBLIC EDUCATION EVEN HAVE A PURPOSE?

Such a silly question! Everyone knows the primary purpose of traditional public education is learning. A quick glance at US history seems to confirm this notion.

No less a guiding light than the father of US public education, Horace Mann (1839), wrote that the purpose of newly minted public, or common, schools in Massachusetts was that "every child born within its borders shall be enlightened" (47).

Historically, state constitutions established public education where learning was the goal to advance the general welfare, ensure economic growth, and foster citizenship participation (Swensson, Ellis, and Shaffer, 2019a). Learning (represented here in California's constitution) was instrumental in "the promotion of 'intellectual, scientific, moral, and agricultural improvement'" (Brighouse and Mullane, 2018, 1).

There is long-standing agreement that "improvement of *student academic outcomes* (Bamburg & Andrews, 1990; Glasman, 1984; Goldring & Pasternak, 1994; Hallinger & Murphy, 1986; Heck et al., 1990; Leithwood, Begley, and Cousins, 1990; Leitner, 1994; O'Day, 1983)" (emphasis original) (Hallinger, 2005, 4) is the primary purpose of public education.

Learning has a societal and individual value. When individuals learn, the general welfare advances. When the general welfare advances (e.g., economic growth, citizenship participation), individuals and society improve. The gravitas of history tips conventional wisdom in the direction of learning for the common good as the primary purpose of America's schools.

A Different Perspective About Purpose

Learning and the common good expressed as the balance between individual rights and the needs of society, however, are not sole point of view about the primary purpose of public education. From the beginning, the primary purpose of public education headed in two different directions.

For instance, when Mann put learning into focus as the primary purpose for public education, state politicians diverted attention away from this function. The first public schools, politicians declared, "should focus more on developing children's character than on increasing their academic knowledge beyond basic literacy and numeracy" (Goldstein, 2015, 27).

Despite this tug-of-war, public educators responded gamely with a sustained focus on learning. The effect of maintaining an eye on this "prize," from a broad historical perspective, was that learning fulfilled the common good of citizenship in US democracy.

Until the middle of the twentieth century.

That was when the struggle over choice about learning and the common good as primary purpose in public education roared on to center stage. Under the guise of reform of the purpose for America's traditional public education, critics threw down the gauntlet (Friedman, 1955; National Commission on Excellence in Education, 1983; Chubb and Moe, 1990).

What's History Got to Do with It?

History, as scholars have pointed out, is not merely an inventory of past events, experiences, and decisions. Rather, history is a storyline edited by present-day circumstances to explain and promote contemporary perspectives (Otremba, 2020).

Otremba (2020) observes that, in this way, history is "a series of *narratives* we tell ourselves . . . [that] function to help define and support present identities and paradigms" (emphasis original) (709). Public education's narrative, then, is history utilized to reflect the intentions and concerns of actors and entities in the present day. History is reconstituted to validate present-day interpretations about US schooling.

EDUCATION AND THE ROLE OF THE PUBLIC SECTOR

Two major perspectives—*traditional US public education* and *privatization education*—emerge as present-day narratives for America's schooling. How contemporary public educators choose a storyline for teaching and learning will be the history edited to validate future identities and paradigms for public education.

Although public education played no role in America's public sector until the 1830s, the major perspectives mirror momentous differences over the role of the public sector that arose during the nation's early history. The role of the public sector in the United States has been a matter of contention since the end of the Revolutionary War.

The Public Sector, Choice, and Preference Substitution

Simply put, the role of the public sector "is 'to provide necessary goods and services to the general public (Jung, 2018, 100)'" (Swensson, Lehman, and Ellis, 2021, 79). From this down-to-earth summary, Americans managed to adopt divergent views about the role of the public sector.

Preference substitution accounts for this bifurcation. "Preference substitution occurs when different institutions or actors in a market for public goods or services value different dimensions of that good or service—when they define 'quality' differently" (Carlson, Cowen, and Fleming, 2013, 902).

As this discussion will reveal, different definitions of "quality" lie at the core of America's struggle over choice about learning. The narrative written in the twenty-first century for the history of the future of public education— represented by either traditional US public education or privatization education—will depend on which definition of quality becomes socially valuable.

The assumption about quality embedded in privatization education, for instance, is that "if the current [public school] system does, indeed, provide education to children inefficiently, then by increasing choice (which should induce competition), one can, theoretically, improve student achievement without significantly increasing public expenditures" (Rouse and Barrow, 2008, 1).

Embracing America's first instinct about the role of the public sector in America, privatization education proponents in the twenty-first century assume (1) that public education does not provide services that align with the tenets of free market theory and that (2) efficiency, low-cost, and competition, in the form of choice education, exemplify the preferable role for education in the public sector.

America's Public Sector: The First Instinct

America's first instinct about the role of the public sector after the Revolutionary War (e.g., the Articles of Confederation) was to enshrine less government, loose public connections, and primacy of individual states (Chernow, 2004; Swensson, Lehman, and Ellis, 2021).

Instead of a tight weave between a national government and the thirteen states, the role of the public sector under the Articles of Confederation took the form of macramé.

"The Articles of Confederation promised little more than a fragile alliance of thirteen miniature republics" (Chernow, 2004, 157). The new nation was rent by schisms: sectionalism vs. nationalism, urban vs. rural, federalist vs. antifederalist, North vs. South (Chernow, 2004).

Weak and dysfunctional, the role of the public sector under the Articles of Confederation was so minimal that states clung to their sovereignty and disputed with other states over innumerable issues. The national government was left to wallow in its own ineptitude.

The Role of the Public Sector: On Second Thought

Widespread and disruptive, the failures of the Articles of Confederation led to a reconsideration of the role of the public sector in terms of governmental structure, the nature of the common good, and a balance of powers between national and state governments. From this extensive reconsideration, a different narrative for the role of America's public sector arose: the US Constitution.

The US Constitution turned away from the societal and governmental disconnections in the Articles of Confederation. Within the US Constitution balance was sought between the power of a unified national government and powers associated with each state.

The Constitution, taking its cue from other documents at the foundation of US democracy, laid the groundwork for the theoretical underpinnings of justice for all and the common good as the role of America's public sector. "'Even in its fledgling beginning where few take part, the idea it represents is one of universal access'" (Knight Abowitz, 2008, 359).

Fate, then Public School

While the role of the public sector played out on the national stage, schooling attracted little attention. Between the early days of the American colonies and the first common or public schools in the mid-1800s, learning was as much an individual's fate as anything else.

Initially, only the very wealthy in America learned from tutors, much less attended colonial era academies or colleges. Parochial schools established by religious sects in the late 1700s had a limited impact (Hartman, 2005). As such, formal learning was left to happenstance, gender, good fortune, race, and/or family wealth (Goldstein, 2015).

This meant that informal education—e.g., family obligations, apprenticeship training, work, lived experience—was the source of most learning. Intentional, state-funded, formal learning experiences for all children simply didn't exist during America's early decades.

The Advent of Formal Education

With the invention of traditional US public education, learning was transformed. Learning transitioned from the informality of happenstance and luck to a formality that was society's responsibility. Public education took on a role in the public sector.

Two developments fueled the transition to formal public education:

1. The economic growth of America from its agrarian infancy into its industrial adolescence entailed a need for "standardized" workers; and
2. America's escalating struggle to realize in daily life for all citizens the principles espoused in the nation's founding documents (Hartman, 2005).

The Best of Intentions

Universal access to the principles espoused in America's founding documents was the intention of some whose efforts shaped the role of the public sector as the nation made its way into the early decades of the nineteenth century. But, between such intentions and their implementation shadows fell (Eliot, 1925).

Shadows (e.g., privilege, discrimination, power, racism) fell and the best of intentions for America's public sector disappeared. Noble intentions were aspirations withheld from many. Americans (e.g., Native Americans, African Americans, women, religious minorities) were excluded from the public sector.

Traditional public education mirrored the troubled implementation of the common good in the nation at large. Illusions of learning, as a result, are all too prevalent in the narrative for public education.

Pendulums: The Roles of the Public Sector

Never far removed from America's consciousness about the role of the public sector, exclusion, violence, and racism fed numerous examples of the denial of America's intentions. In the second half of the nineteenth century, for instance, the Ordinance of Nullification, the Missouri Compromise, the Know-Nothing Party, the Civil War, *Plessy v. Ferguson*, and Jim Crow sustained America's split personality about the role of the public sector.

A century later, though, the role of the public sector swung toward greater congruence with the common good. From the Civil Rights Movement to the desegregation of public education, from the women's suffrage movement to the War on Poverty, and from The Civil Rights Act of 1964 to the Americans with Disabilities Act, promises, intentions, and aspirations lingering in the shadows for more than two centuries inched forward.

The rise and fall, the back-and-forth, of the role of the public sector contributes to the contemporary tumult over public education (e.g., segregation academies, curriculum skirmishes, funding insufficiencies). US history, the role of the public sector, and the two major perspectives about public education are integral to the narrative about public schooling and its purpose in the twenty-first century, and beyond.

THE PURPOSE OF STRUGGLE OVER PURPOSE

The purpose of the struggle over purpose in US public education is control of public education. The purpose of the struggle over purpose is divided:

- Either, the struggle over purpose is an attempt to leverage financial, ideological, and political issues that attend public schooling as the narrative for choice about learning for the future role of US public education.
- Or, the struggle over purpose is an attempt to write the narrative about the role of America's public schools that facilitates choice about learning *how to think* on behalf of the common good for all US students.

Incomplete: Public Sector and Public Education

For more than two centuries, intentions about the role of the public sector linked to justice for all are, at best, incomplete and, at worst, moribund.

The depth of this problem for public education and the rest of America's public sector is described succinctly by Knight Abowitz (2008) when she observes that "since 'cultural' has historically meant 'different' in U.S. society, 'full citizenship and cultural visibility appear to be inversely related'" (370).

Traditional US public education mirrors the incomplete freedoms and denial of rights infesting the role of the public sector despite the promises and potential in the language of America's founding documents. America's public education and its purpose pendulum in rhythm with these failures and limited successes.

Contemporary US public education is subject to narratives that define and support the identities and paradigms and purposes of two major perspectives. History, as it evolves into a future, provides public educators with choices that become narratives for purpose.

Claimants from each major perspective about US education contend over purpose via contemporary narratives to control the future of education in America. If public educators recognize the differences embedded in these narratives, then the struggle over choice of the purpose that controls learning will pit student-centric intentions against adult-centric intentions.

INTO THE BREACH: PUBLIC EDUCATORS, INTENTIONS, AND INSTRUMENTAL AGENCY

The history of public education, the role of the public sector in America, the societal battlegrounds that impinge upon teaching and learning—all are part of the contemporary struggle over choice of the primary purpose in US education. It often appears that influencing this narrative is beyond the capacities of traditional public educators.

Where Future Purpose Starts

Appearances, however, are deceiving. Public educators have access to tools capable of choice for purpose throughout America's schooling: *instrumental agency* and *praxis*.

Instrumental agency is "a tool to do something socially valuable and pre-defined in advance" (Matusov, von Duyke, and Kayumova, 2016, 426).

Praxis, "the continual interplay between reflection and action" (Furman, 2012, 197), facilitates consideration of predefined socially valuable action. "Praxis must involve not only study and self-reflection, but also a 'conscious-ness of our incompleteness' which leads to 'rigorous curiosity' and 'motivates our searching and inquiry' (pp. 127–128)" (Furman, 2012, 7).

For public educators, praxis incorporates *good thinking*, which is "the tendency to identify and investigate problems, to probe assumptions, to seek reasons, and to be reflective" (Perkins and Tishman, 2016). Praxis fuels the instrumental agency of public educators to enact intentions. *Intentions* are designs to do things that are socially valuable and natural to education.

A Split Screen

The contemporary narrative about the disparate intentions of the two major perspectives about public education offers a split-screen presentation about what is socially valuable. The two major perspectives embrace contrasting intentions.

Praxis and instrumental agency, as a result, can lead in diametrically opposite directions. What is natural to public education, thus, is rendered problematic.

The struggle over control, the battle over the purpose of purpose in US public education, hinges on how public educators reflect and act upon intentions.

US EDUCATION: BUILDING A FUTURE

Like a hammer, instrumental agency is a dual-purpose tool. The weighted end of a hammer drives nails to connect and build. The claw end of a hammer disconnects and pulls apart.

Instrumental agency functions, like a hammer, to connect or pull apart. Authorities, educators, ideologues, scholars, and citizens in the twenty-first century have a choice: Either apply instrumental agency to build or to pull apart.

Instrumental agency can be employed to create either traditional US public education, or privatization/choice education as the future for teaching and learning in America (Swensson, Ellis, and Shaffer, 2019a; Swensson, Lehman, and Ellis, 2021; Swensson and Shaffer, 2020).

These perspectives are built from radically different designs for predefined things that are socially valuable. Each perspective is constructed by separate intentions, and these intentions identify ends and means associated with a unique view of the primary purpose of public education.

This division has its origin in the fraught role of the public sector throughout US history and forces public educators to confront a future that cannot travel in opposite directions at the same time.

Understanding that one of the major perspectives clings to tenets that mirror the role of the public sector under the Articles of Confederation and understanding that the other major perspective offers public education aligned with the role of the public sector under the US Constitution is a platform from which public educators can engage actively with choices about the future of teaching and learning.

Primary Purpose in Moments and Lessons

The major perspectives about US education convey different relationships between end purposes and the means of attaining these purposes. The means that yield each perspective incorporate reflection and instrumental agency about intentions. Purpose is the predefined socially valuable end state fostered by each perspective, the means to an end state are identified in this discussion as *learnable moments* or *inconvenient lessons.*

Learnable Moments

Reflection and action identify *learnable moments* from history, policy, precedent, theory, practice, scholarship, legislation, and/or expectation that fulfill the relationship between means and ends in a major perspective.

Learnable moments that encompass *student-centric intentions* are non-negotiable drivers of instrumental agency for traditional US public education (Swensson, Ellis, and Shaffer, 2019b). For instance, designs at the core of traditional US public education represent the premise that schools are "all things to all people by virtue of their open and equitable employment and enrollment guidelines" (Stitzlein, 2015, 565).

Learnable moments that encompass *adult-centric intentions* are the non-negotiable drivers of instrumental agency in privatization education (Swensson, Ellis, and Shaffer, 2019a).

For example, adult-centric designs for privatization education represent the premise that "school choice programs diminish monopoly power held by traditional public school leaders and, therefore, lead to increased overall quality levels and lower costs (Chubb and Moe, 1990; Friedman and Friedman, 1990)" (DeAngelis and Erickson, 2018, 250).

INCONVENIENT LESSONS

Reflection and action reject *inconvenient lessons* from history, policy, precedent, theory, practice, scholarship, legislation, and/or expectation that are antithetical to the relationship between means and ends in each major perspective. Praxis is sufficient to determine inconvenient lessons that are not socially valuable.

Lessons Rejected: Traditional Public Education

Adherents of traditional US public education reject inconvenient lessons such as:

- *Free market theory*. At its core, free market theory "denies the importance of public goods or else maintains that all our goods are best achieved by individuals acting out of individual self-interest" (Hostetler, 2003, 355). Policy, history, practice, legislation, and expectation derived from free market theory do not fulfill student-centric intentions and, therefore, are rejected as inconvenient lessons by proponents of traditional US public education.

  Intentions of free market theory are rejected for several reasons: (1) marketplaces are amoral (Lubienski, 2013); (2) traditional US public education does not constitute "the pure markets idealized by some thinkers" (Lubienski, Gulosino, and Weitzel, 2009, 605); and (3) the implementation of privatization mechanisms (e.g., charter schools, vouchers, education savings plans, virtual schools) diverts state funding from traditional public schools (Hefling, 2017, 6).

- *Singularity.* Singularity is exclusion of *the public* and the prioritization of selected individuals. When free market theory prioritizes selected individuals as socially valuable to the detriment of the common good, citizenship in US democracy deteriorates. Segregation, privileged enrollment practices, hidden fees—all are rivalrous and exclusionary characteristics of free market schooling aided and abetted by singularity (Bolsen, 2013). Singularity is rejected by advocates of traditional public education because it yields state discrimination, social engineering, and escape to bigotry (Swensson, Ellis, and Shaffer, 2019a, 99–102).
- *Efficiency and Cost Avoidance.* Efficiency is an intention fulfilled by the selection of "mechanisms [that] are heralded for low cost and the delivery of hallmarks of free market theory: lower taxation, less government, and competition between schools in a marketplace" (Swensson, Lehman, and Ellis, 2021, 52).

    Laissez-faire regulatory environments and state statutes are means that nurture educational marketplaces (Wong and Shen, 2006) where efficiency and cost avoidance are among the adult-centric intentions responsible for underfunding traditional public education (Swensson, Lehman, and Ellis, 2021).

    The alignment between mechanisms and adult-centric intentions is so complete that privatization education proponents equate mechanisms with education (Swensson, Lehman, and Ellis, 2021). Mechanisms align elegantly with the intentions of free market theory which are "characterized by faith in economic determinism, acquisitive individualism, entitlement ethics, and meritocracy" (Kurth-Schai, 2014, 423).
- *Profit.* Profit represents one fiscal aspect of ROI (Return on Investment) in free market education. Profit, one adult-centric intention of privatization education, overturns the responsibility of US public education for the welfare of all students.

    Overall, "ROI embodies the premise that efficiency, profit, and low-cost government are the fiduciary, adult-centric returns expected when society invests in adult-centric advantages to establish public education" (Swensson and Shaffer, 2020, 44). Profit and the other attributes of ROI counteract two responsibilities accepted by traditional public educators.

    Public educators accept responsibilities for developing in all "young people both the knowledge and skills that individuals need to live free lives and the shared values . . . that citizens need to support the institutions that enable them to live freely" (Gutmann and Ben-Porath, 2015, 1).

Profit is rejected by traditional public education as inconsistent with accountability for something greater than self and as the antithesis of the obligation to serve all future citizens in US democracy.

Lessons Rejected: Privatization Education

Privatization education rejects inconvenient lessons such as:

- *The Common Good*. The common good is a student-centric intention rejected by privatization education in favor of the good of the individual (i.e., singularity). Privatization education aligned with free market theory "views education as only an individual experience sought to fulfill one's unique desires" (Knight Abowitz and Stitzlein, 2018, 34).

  The learnable moments selected for privatization education are those aligned with the premise that "education strongly affects the future economic returns that individuals see" (Hanushek, 2020, 1).

  Self-aggrandizement, "the good" as singularity, is maximized in free market education. Proponents of privatization schooling intend that a good school "will affirm their own social, political, and increasingly, even religious worldviews" (Stitzlein, 2015, 565). Free market theory proponents reject the common good as expensive and inefficient because it "is something that cannot feasibly be withheld from others in a group if it is provided for any member of that group (Olson 1965)" (Bolsen, 2013, 2).

  The common good is an inconvenient lesson because it rejects singularity. Further, the common good does not depend on survival of the fittest embedded in competition at the core of the educational marketplace.

- *Investment*. "Free market theory holds that education is (1) a cost, not an investment and (2) an individual good, not a public or common good" (Swensson, Lehman, and Ellis, 2021, 52). Fiscal investment in traditional public education that strives for RTS (Return to Students) is rejected.

  Instead, cost reduction and efficiency are learnable moments. These adult-centric intentions are invoked in policy designed so that effective teachers receive "extra pay to accept larger class sizes (a trade-off that many teachers indicate they are willing to take), the higher pay becomes extra pay for extra work—and more students are taught by the best teachers" (Hanushek, 2020, 10).

  Investment in public education is rejected "because the price to acquire the public good means giving up the primacy of self-interest lying at the core of privatization" (Swensson, Ellis, and Shaffer, 2019a, 83).

- *Traditional US public education.* Privatization education adherents reject traditional public education as an inconvenient lesson because it is "a rule-laden, risk-averse sector dominated by entrenched bureaucracies, industrial style collective-bargaining agreements, and hoary colleges of education" (Hess, 2010, 47).

Free market theory intends "that schools (public sector) should be run like businesses (private sector), [which] while lacking any evidentiary warrant, has become a new 'common sense' among a wide swath of the American public (Cuban, 2004; Goodsell, 2004; Mautner, 2010)" (Anderson and Donchik, 2016, 337).

Traditional US public education is rejected when free market proponents "increasingly cast public schools in formalistic terms—categorizing them by their form, rather than their function—while trimming those terms to better align with their own structure" (Stitzlein, 2017, 1/3).

Traditional US public education is rejected because its intentions are the antithesis of free market forms such as the educational marketplace and mechanisms in the market.

DeAngelis and Erickson (2018) share a justification for rejecting the intentions of traditional public education when they observe that "if the definition of quality is unique to each individual, we could say that the school selection itself—the student-school match—is the definition of quality" (251).

Privatization education, promoted from the 1990s into the twenty-first century, is touted by proponents "as cutting edge and a significant catalyst for redefining the traditional landscape of the American public school system" (Gallo, 2014, 209–210).

Adherents of free market schooling, for instance, indicate that "school choice programs diminish monopoly power held by traditional public school leaders and, therefore, lead to increased overall quality levels and lower costs (Chubb and Moe, 1990; Friedman and Friedman, 1990)" (DeAngelis and Erickson, 2018, 250).

Purpose, *the Public*, and Perspectives

What is predefined and socially valuable in America's education depends on the learnable moments and inconvenient lessons identified by the proponents of each perspective.

These notions configure the narrative for the future of learning and the common good. Educators and others concerned with US education engage in metaphorical combat and intentions are among the weapons of choice.

Predefined, intentions and identification of what is and is not socially valuable maneuver America's education toward different pathways. Choosing between these roads commits teaching and learning to a dead end or to a continuous journey.

Chapter 2

Which Road for Public Education?

EMAIL
To: Traditional Public Educators
Fr: Team 7A
Re: Robert Frost to the Rescue

Teaching is hard work. Learning is hard work. Traditional US public education is the collaborative effort (i.e., educators + parents/caregivers + the public/government) to focus this hard work on engaging all students with meaningful futures.

Every public educator knows, however, that the disparate perspectives on schooling in America constitute a fork in the road. The choice that lies in front of contemporary public educators mirrors the dilemma faced by a traveler in "The Road Not Taken" (Frost, 1942).

The roads that lie in front of America's public educators are paved with either *adult-centric intentions* or *student-centric intentions.* Each set of intentions discussed in the upcoming chapter prompts a choice of either a *destination* (i.e., privatization education) or a *journey* (i.e., traditional US public education) for learning.

As the next chapter illustrates, choice can lead authorities, legislators, and educators to adopt justifications for intentions that result in inconsequential student achievement and insufficient financial support for public schools. Self-serving and self-affirming modes of thinking—*my-side bias* and *synergy of struggle*—support choice for learning nurtured by self-aggrandizing comfort zones.

It is possible, in this way, to rely solely on intentions to choose the purpose or function of US schooling. This instrumental agency assigns social value to *stasis* and *singularity* aligned with free market theory.

In the next chapter, *arbiters of choice* reveal the contrast between the intentions of the major perspectives. Arbiters of choice convey the implications and consequences of reflection and action that help narrate the history of the future of US public education: *form vs. function*; *accountability to vs. accountability for*; *given responsibility vs. responsibility accepted*; *and burden vs. obligation*.

These four duos illuminate the extent to which the road taken and the road not taken by public educators will determine the future of teaching and learning in America.

CHOOSING THE ROAD TO THE FUTURE OF PUBLIC EDUCATION

Robert Frost gives voice in "The Road Not Taken" (1942) to the inescapable choice that arises when a traveler comes to a fork in the road.

Like the traveler in Frost's poem, public educators in the twenty-first century confront an inescapable choice. Choosing one of the two major perspectives about education will determine the future of teaching and learning in America.

Frost's traveler notices little difference between the roads that lie ahead and observes that "the passing there had worn them really about the same" (Frost, 1942, 131). The same cannot be said about the roads that lie before public educators. The two major perspectives about America's education are worn quite differently.

The intentions that generate each perspective account for these differences. The aggregate effect of adult-centric intentions is the destination of learning in US education. The aggregate effect of student-centric intentions is a continuing journey of learning in US education.

Intending a destination or a journey, public educators will choose a road to the history of the future of public education that "made all the difference" (Frost, 1942, 131).

PUBLIC EDUCATION: JOURNEY OR DESTINATION?

A journey and a destination are not the same. Disparate intentions, and the significant differences between the two major perspectives about US education, are captured in terminology that defines elements central to the struggle over purpose (see Textbox 2.1). Choosing one perspective or the other is a contemporary, difficult, and contentious task.

For those who play a role in choosing a perspective that serves as the history of the future of public education, recognition of these difficulties is a resource of considerable value. Resolving the question about the primary purpose of US public education ought to involve reflection and action about the social value of either adult-centric intentions or student-centric intentions. For public educators, reflection and action can begin with an examination of the implications and consequences of intentions for US education illustrated in *arbiters of choice.*

TEXTBOX 2.1

Relevant Terminology

Instrumental Agency:	*"A tool to do something socially valuable and predefined in advance"* (Matusov, von Duyke, and Kayumova, 2016, 426).
Intentions:	*Designs to do things that are socially valuable and natural to education.*
My-side Bias:	*The human tendency to justify choices via self-serving rationalizations.* (Molden and Higgins, 2012)
Singularity:	*Exclusion of the public and the prioritization of selected individuals. "Singularity (thinking and acting exclusively for self-aggrandizement of individuals or cohorts) excludes 'the other'"* (Swensson and Lehman, 2021, 98).
Synergy of Struggle:	*Permits adherents of a perspective to experience "emotional depth as well as the intellectual satisfaction that springs from the transformation of uncertainty, ambivalence, and complexity into an understandable phenomenon (Edelman, 1988, 40)"* (Granger, 2008, 212).
Teaching:	*Teaching is "the power to lead-out student intelligences with knowledge, cognitive process, and/or skills beyond their personal assets"* (Swensson and Lehman, 2021, 57).
Virtue	*"Virtue or arête is an excellence that encompasses both ethics and competency"* (Ciulla, et al., 2018, 5).

ARBITERS OF CHOICE

Intentions comprise each major perspective. Which intentions, however, are socially valuable? When US public educators determine which intentions are socially valuable, they write the history of the future of US public education.

Under these circumstances, choice in US education takes on a new dimension.

This dimension of choice takes educators beyond mere selection of one school or another and to choosing a commitment to instrumental agency necessary and sufficient to the journey represented by student-centric intentions or the destination represented by adult-centric intentions.

Educational choice in the twenty-first century is layered with the intentions of each major perspective. Intentions, thus, are *arbiters of choice* for the narrative about purpose in the future of US education.

Choosing Between Intentions

Defining features of each major perspective, intentions surround and influence public educators.

Often, public educators are unaware of the influence of one set of intentions or the other. Public educators can be oblivious because their time and attention are taken up by "the uncertainty, turbulence, messiness, and unpredictability of the milieu of schooling" (Goldring and Greenfield, 2002, 2).

But public educators cannot afford to ignore arbiters of choice. The reason that traditional public educators are obliged to understand intentions, choice, and perspectives is that the road taken by the narrative about the history of the future of public education can be chosen without public educator input.

Numerous other interested parties (e.g., ideologues, legislators, state officials) are poised to fill any vacuum created if public educators are uninvolved with choice about learning and the narrative it creates for the future.

Duos: Intentions of the Major Perspectives

To engage meaningfully with choice, the social value of the intentions for each perspective needs to be examined. Four duos suggest the contrasts that develop from intentions:

- Form *vs.* Function
- Accountability to free market theory *vs.* Accountability for all students
- Responsibility given *vs.* Responsibility accepted
- Burden *vs.* Obligation

Labels on the left side of each duo summarize the intentions of privatization education. Labels on the right side summarize the intentions of traditional US public education.

How public educators interpret the implications and consequences of the intentions framed by arbiters of choice is not a scholarly enterprise devoid of connection with the lives of students and the progress of US democracy. The choice made about the road taken has a direct effect on the life-costs paid by too many US students.

THE LIFE-COSTS THAT US STUDENTS PAY

Arbiters of choice point the way to the destination of privatization education or to the journey of traditional US public education.

Before examining the differences embedded in the arbiters of choice, it is critical to call attention to America's students. Students, after all, will occupy classrooms, experience instruction, and emerge with learning dependent on the narrative chosen for teaching and learning.

One measure of the intentions linked with each perspective is the extent to which privatization education and traditional public education can exert a positive influence on learning to reduce the life-costs exacted on too many of America's students.

The Life-Cost of Poverty

Poverty sits beside too many of the almost 77 million US students enrolled in traditional public schools. Poverty also accompanies some of the 3.2 million students enrolled in charter schools, as of the 2017–2018 school year (Gilblom and Sang, 2019). More than 50 percent of K-12 public school students are "eligible to receive free or reduced-price lunch" (Suitts, 2016, 36).

Poverty weighs heavily on students and the schools they attend. The enduring toll of poverty is visited with punishing impact on students of color. "Sixty percent of black and Hispanic students attend majority poor schools, while only 30% of Asian students and only 18% of white students do so" (Orfield and Lee, as cited in Logan and Burdick-Will, 2015, 324).

"High rates of student poverty have a significant impact on the levels and types of resources, and the funding needed, to give those students a meaningful opportunity for success in school" (Farrie, Kim, and Sciarra, 2019, 12). Baker, Farrie, and Sciarra, (2016) reveal the desperate, long-term, learning implications of poverty: an *income-based achievement gap* that is "nearly twice as large as the Black-White achievement gap" (2).

The Life-Cost of Racism

Rector-Aranda (2016) defines racism as "an uncritical habit of mind (including perceptions, attitudes, assumptions, and beliefs) that justifies inequity and exploitation by accepting the existing order of things as given" (3). "A long-standing stain on the nation's promises, racism plagues US education (Suitts, 2019; Weathers and Sosina, 2019)" (Swensson, Lehman, and Ellis, 2021, 83).

Racism infests beliefs, decisions, and actions in US education to the point that the existing order of things as given can consent "to the argument that because students from impoverished homes are unlikely to benefit from a 'quality' education, funding public schools equally in rich and poor neighborhoods would only waste tax dollars" (Biddle and Berliner, 2002, 54).

Blatant discrimination like this doubles down via statutes that assure "the prevalence of resegregation and the resultant inequality caused by school choice" (Dawkins-Law, 2014, 3). This devastating order of things as given also includes the lie of race-based intellectual inferiority, which "stands as one of the most demeaning, false, and damaging examples of racism to afflict US public education" (Swensson and Shaffer, 2020, 23).

WHEN CHOICE IS SELF-SATISFACTION

Choosing what is socially valuable and natural to education does not need to be difficult or complicated if choice is nothing more than idiosyncratic or personalized preferences supported by *my-side bias* and *synergy of struggle.*

Choosing to Satisfy "Me"

My-side bias (Molden and Higgins, 2012), is the human tendency to justify choices simply because they are self-serving. My-side bias is the cognitive and emotional tunnel vision that "gravitates to ideas, interests, or points of view that reflect only an individual's own perspective" (Swensson, Ellis, and Shaffer, 2019b, 60).

My-side bias provides a foundation for substitution preference. My-side bias allows "me" to be the center of decisions and justification for decisions.

"My-side bias, thinking riveted to the validation of self-interest, obviates the need to understand different ideas or different points of view" (Swensson, Ellis, and Shaffer, 2019b, 60). My-side bias is an individual's wherewithal to render data, evidence, and/or information into self-justification.

My-side bias is self-justification of self-selected points of view that fuels and sustains *us vs. them* competition.

Synergy of struggle (Granger, 2008) permits adherents of a perspective to experience "'emotional depth as well as the intellectual satisfaction that springs from the transformation of uncertainty, ambivalence, and complexity into an understandable phenomenon' (Edelman, 1988, p. 40)" (Granger, 2008, 212).

Synergy of struggle segues with my-side bias into an emotionally satisfying phenomenon whereby individuals embrace right-makes-right to simplify and justify choice. My-side bias and synergy of struggle supply the emotional concrete to frame and solidify *comfort zones*.

In combination, synergy of struggle and my-side bias provide legislators, state officials, educators, citizens, and ideologues with the means to ignore intentions divorced from their self-interest. The self-explanatory value of these tools of self-justification validate adult-centric intentions and, thus, simplify the choice for a road taken to the future of US education.

Defending a perspective by asserting its social value as a matter of personal aggrandizement enshrines disconnection from learning.

SINGULARITY: THE ME, MYSELF, AND I FOR EDUCATION'S FUTURE

My-side bias and synergy of struggle nurture a bunker mentality that rivets US public education to a free market destination. Enclosed in this self-affirming echo chamber, reflection and action are limited to identifying singularity as socially valuable.

Singularity "refers to the moral obligation to pursue the contemporary purpose of education because it fulfills the self-interest of individuals" (Swensson and Shaffer, 2020, 15). "Singularity is the expectation of privatization that the needs of individuals outweigh the greater good" (Swensson and Lehman, 2021, 135).

Singularity brings an essential, retrograde, premise of free market theory into schools and classrooms. From singularity, "marketplace adherents see additional benefits in that 'students are taught to see themselves as being in competition with others for scarce opportunities and goods' (Strike, 2008, p. 121)" (Swensson and Shaffer, 2020, 31).

The singularity focus of free market theory instills the belief that "relatively few people are likely to spend time and resources making sure that someone else's education (or health care or justice) is adequate" (Shaw, 2010, 242). Education identified as a responsibility to fulfill only individual desires constitutes the rejection of education as a greater, public, good.

Free market schooling embraces the marketplace premise that "big was assumed to be better than small; getting more was preferable to getting less" (Cameron and McNaughtan, 2014, 448). Growth is perceived as an essential ingredient in the recipe for organizational effectiveness (Whetten, 1980, 578). Growth becomes a prime objective of proponents of free market education.

Growth is self-aggrandizement in this marketplace. Ideological self-interest and/or financial self-interest are targeted for growth by proponents of free market schooling. Singularity and competition generate goals, tactics, and outcomes essential to marketplace success.

Growing the common good takes a back seat to increasing the number of privatization schools and students on behalf of profit, low taxation, and less government. Growth of ideological engagement instead of achievement growth for all students is the priority of marketplace schooling.

"Singularity, in this sense, distorts what scholars refer to as 'the special human capacity for "theory of mind" [which] allows us to appreciate that we may have different perspectives and concerns' (Mercer, 2013, p. 163)" (Swensson and Shaffer, 2020, 32). Traditional public education advocates gain no traction toward the destination of learning as an individual's ideological proclivities.

MAKING SENSE OF THE BATTLE LINES
BETWEEN PERSPECTIVES

Battle lines are drawn in US education between perspectives. Disparate purposes, intentions, and outcomes are reflected in the divisions represented in the arbiters of choice.

The role of public educators in the twenty-first century, thus, is to make sense out of these divisions in terms of their impact on students and society. The history of the future of traditional US public education will emerge when the instrumental agency of public educators incorporates this meaning-making.

Understanding Intentions Via the Arbiters of Choice

Enthusiastic actors on the broad stage of US public education are ready to choose a destination for the future of teaching and learning. Legislators, ideologues, state authorities, pundits, and citizens have demonstrated their eagerness to identify self-serving intentions as socially valuable and, thus, to control the future of America's education.

Such enthusiasm spotlights the imperative for analysis of the arbiters of choice. Taking a step forward in the next chapter, this discussion turns to a question that public educators must answer in relationship to the first arbiter of choice: *Will form follow function or will function follow form in the learning lives of US students?*

Chapter 3

Arbiters of Choice

Form vs. Function

EMAIL
To: Traditional Public Educators
Fr: Colleagues in the 3rd Grade Pod
Re: Following the Leader

Begin with the end in mind. Sound advice for all educators that echoes the axiom coined by US architect, Louis Sullivan: *form follows function.*

These phrases spotlight the importance of purpose or function as the guiding light for public educators. Form is determined after purpose.

Unfortunately, legislators, ideologues, state authorities, and others turn this advice inside out. When this happens, *function follows form* and structures mandates, statutes, and ideologies for public education.

In the upcoming chapter, *form* vs. *function* is shared as the first of four arbiters of choice. The intentions in this, and every, duo offer public educators insights into the nature of the future for learning intended through each major perspective.

The contrast between these intentions—form and function—could not be more stark. When form follows function, on the one hand, *virtue, the original power of education, the public good* are socially valuable. If function follows form, on the other hand, *choice, mechanisms, Return on Investment* become socially valuable.

So definitive is the contrast between *form follows function* and *function follows form* that prioritizing one over the other steps in the direction of a road taken and steps away from a road not taken for the future of teaching and learning in America.

Form, for example, is a choice to step in the direction of *adult-centric intentions* (e.g., competition, low-cost, efficiency), *mechanisms* (e.g.,

25

charter schools, vouchers, tax credits, virtual education), and *ROI* (Return on Investment).

Function or purpose is a step in the direction of *student-centric intentions* (e.g., *how to think,* the common good, *the public*), dynamic instruction, and RTS (Return to Students).

In the depth and breadth of the contrasts represented by form vs. function, lies an illustration of the importance of choice about the future of America's teaching and learning. Prioritizing function or prioritizing form, public educators initiate the narrative for the history of the future of US public education.

THE ARCHITECTURE OF INTENTIONS

Late in the nineteenth century, renowned America architect Louis Sullivan summarized his professional intentions with what has become a well-known axiom: *form follows function* (Sullivan, 1896). Sullivan's axiom asserts that the purpose of something, aka its function, determines the form it takes.

"Function is activity that is natural to something. A reasonable person could readily identify activities natural to public education—teaching, learning, leading" (Swensson and Lehman, 2021, 44).

The value of prioritizing what is natural to public education, for instance, is central to planning instruction. Contemporary echoes of Sullivan's original statement resonate in Covey's (2020) advice to *begin with the end in mind.*

With the rise of privatization education, however, form follows function becomes an inconvenient lesson. Under these circumstances, adult-centric intentions prioritize form, and Sullivan's phrase is reversed: *function follows form.*

Sullivan's axiom and the inverse of the axiom are contradictions. What is socially valuable if form follows function and what is socially valuable if function follows form are diametrically opposed. Thus, *form* vs. *function* is an arbiter of choice. The contradictions within this arbiter of choice offer a conundrum that public educators ignore at the peril of a narrative in education based on a student-centric purpose.

What Is Socially Valuable if *Form* Follows *Function*?

When form follows function, purpose is represented in things socially valuable and natural to traditional US public education such as:

- *Virtue:* "Virtue or *arête* is an excellence that encompasses both ethics and competency" (Ciulla, Knights, Mabey, and Tomkins, 2018, 5).

Competency is synopsized by Ritchart and Perkins (2005), who write that "it is not enough to simply consume predigested knowledge, one must also become a knowledge builder (Scandamalia, Bereiter, and Lamon, 1994) and problem solver (Polya, 1957; Schoenfeld, 1982; Selz, 1935)" (777).

Ethics "is concerned with the kinds of values and morals an individual or society finds desirable or appropriate. Furthermore, ethics is concerned with the virtuousness of individuals and their motives" (Northouse, 2007, 342).

Knight Abowitz (2008) summarizes ethics for education in a democracy: "Schools are to help build the civic capacities and a wider sense of common good among diverse students and families" (360).

In combination, ethics and competency are virtue, which is "deeply rooted in responsibility involving imagination and ability to see other viewpoints; willingness to judge for oneself; and willingness to act, and to pay for these actions, if need be" (Ciulla, Knights, Maybe, and Tomkins, 2018, 9).

- *The original power of education:* The original power of education is the exchange of intelligences between teacher and student (Biesta, 2009). "The original power of education occurs in the dialectic between teaching and learning. 'This exchange occurs during classroom construction of the intersection of *how to think* and the moral obligation of public education' (Swensson and Shaffer, 2020, p. 67)" (Swensson and Lehman, 2021, 57).

- *Public good:* Enacted in schools supported by state and local funding, public education in US democracy is a *public good*, one of those "things that benefit everyone but which no one has an individual incentive to provide" (Bolsen, 2013, 1). Traditional public education intends the public, or common, good for every citizen.

What Is Socially Valuable if *Function* Follows *Form*?

When function follows form, purpose is represented in things that are socially valuable and natural to privatization education including:

- *Choice:* School choice is a form that gives "some measure of independence from state and district regulations in exchange for accountability to increase student achievement (Kolderie 1990)" (Stein, 2015, 599). Choice education is a socially valuable learnable moment because it guarantees parents and caregivers "publicly funded, privately operated schools that families can select outside of their zoned [traditional public] schools" (Loeb, Valant, and Kasman, 2011, 143).

- *Democracy-aversion:* "Rather than the publicly elected school boards that govern traditional public education, choice schools, and particularly the boards that govern charter schools, are 'designed to sidestep the unwieldy directives of democratic school governance' (Green, E., 2018, p. 16; Long, 2018)" (Swensson, Ellis, and Shaffer, 2019b, 68). Singularity, self-aggrandizement, and competition are socially valuable forms prioritized in free market education at the expense of the public good.
- *Mechanisms:* Mechanisms are forms (e.g., vouchers, charter schools, virtual schools) synonymous with privatization education. "Mechanisms, from the perspective of school choice proponents, constitute 'the evidence for successful school choice programs' (DeAngelis and Erickson, 2018, p. 249)" (Swensson and Shaffer, 2020, 30).
- *ROI:* Entities and individuals benefit financially when low-cost forms are operationalized to ensure a "return" from the burden of taxation. Ironically, these forms are referred to as Return on *Investment* (ROI). These returns are the heartbeat of an adult-centric ideology.

ROI is meant to advantage privatization education and its proponents. Observers confirm that a significant consequence of ROI is to "'take public dollars . . . away from the existing public schools, effectively creating a two-tier educational system that could hurt the students most in need' (Rich, 2014)" (Swensson, Ellis, and Shaffer, 2019a, 48).

The tenets of free market theory are a return. "ROI delivers the expectations of its proponents when choice, mechanisms, and the primacy of singularity are the minimums that suffice for educational adequacy" (Swensson and Shaffer, 2020, 45). These forms of ideological purity are rendered socially valuable by incorporating the limitations and restrictions endemic to marketplace education:

> The invisible hand—or the power of market forces—is able to influence behavior as it metes out rewards and punishments in a seemingly rational system. It becomes a proxy measure of success, providing an explanation for the failure of the disadvantaged while ensuring that the privileged remain so. (Boesenberg, 2003, 67)

Under these circumstances, the function of education becomes a creature of its form, which becomes its purpose.

PUBLIC EDUCATION: ALREADY ON THE ROAD

America's public education traveled a long way before encountering diverging perspectives. Cubberley (1919), Goldstein (2015), and Urban, Wagner, and Gaither (2019) are among the numerous scholars who describe this trek. The road traveled, in this case, had few off-ramps and significant numbers of potholes, more often than not.

Form and Function Vie for Control

Form or function? Whichever comes first sets the pace for education as a destination or a journey. Choice by public educators to prioritize either function or form will begin to narrate the history of the future in terms aligned with one major perspective.

For example, the choice to prioritize form or function will determine the nature of *teaching** as the instructional activity natural to education.

(**Author's note:* Teaching is defined throughout this narrative as "the power to *lead-out* student intelligences with knowledge, cognitive process, and/or skills beyond their personal assets" [Swensson and Lehman, 2021, 57].)

Choice between form and function will influence the extent to which there is linkage between democracy and public education. The chosen perspective will sustain, or curtail, "a continual struggle for the creation of schools that address relevant societal needs, provide broad access, and, in the last half century, attempt to provide equal opportunity" (Laguardia and Pearl, 2009, 354).

AND SO, BATTLE LINES ARE DRAWN

The struggle over choice about learning begins with educators' instrumental agency to prioritize either form or function. Will purpose, or function, determine the form, what is natural, in public education for the future? Will form supersede function so that adult-centric intentions control teaching and learning?

Public educators who differentiate between the intentions that represent form and the intentions that represent function put themselves in position to prioritize what is natural to US education for the remainder of the twenty-first century. Form vs. function, and the remaining arbiters of choice, put the future of public education into the hands of public educators.

Chapter 4

Arbiters of Choice

Accountability to *vs. Accountability* for

EMAIL
To: Traditional Public Educators
Fr: Your English Department Friends
Re: Waiting for Student-Centric Accountability

Every public educator knows that accountability has infested teaching and learning.

Activated in the form of standardized testing and enforced by negative sanctions, accountability hijacks day-to-day practice in, and the purpose of, traditional public education.

Assessment, at one point in the history of US education, was an educator's way of keeping track of student progress. Accountable for something greater than self, public educators used assessment to respond to the learning of each student.

Accountability, however, has short circuited the power of assessment.

The effect of accountability on America's public education is presented in the upcoming chapter as a pivotal distinction between *to* and *for*. The future of teaching and learning will develop from the choice between:

1. *accountability to* free market theory, or
2. *accountability for* all students (assessment).

The next chapter discusses the different intentions in the arbiter of choice *accountability to* vs. *accountability for* (assessment). Choice between these two will hinge on "valuing [of] *educational* concerns which may or may not lend themselves to measurement—such as thinking and being moral" (Webster, 2017, 333).

31

Replacing professional judgment with data from standardized testing, *accountability to* free market tenets such as efficiency, choice, and singularity turns public education into a commodity. Wedding education to the principles of free market theory, *accountability to* validates competition and preferred customers in an educational marketplace.

Accountability for all students is synonymous with assessment, a public educator's wherewithal to improve learning and grow the meaning-making (e.g., cognitive, creative, and practical capabilities) of all students.

Learning and *accountability to* are the educational equivalent of oil and water because the intentions of free market education are not aligned with student thinking. *Accountability for*, on the other hand, jump-starts the journey sparked by the original power of education.

WHAT HATH ACCOUNTABILITY WROUGHT?

Accountability is a "thing" in public schools. Overtaking assessment in the late twentieth century, accountability—usually in the form of standardized testing—is a creature of ideology promoted as a cure for the maladies, the inconvenient lessons, alleged to afflict traditional US public education (National Commission on Excellence in Education, 1983).

So overwhelming is the imposition of accountability throughout public education—e.g., statutory requirements, sanctions for low scores—that its effects are represented in two developments:

1. evidence of the positive academic impact of traditional public education is overshadowed (Bracey, 2004; 2009).
2. evidence of standardized testing doing "students a disservice, as these kinds of exams are less likely to foster thinking critically and applying knowledge" (Jensen, McDaniel, Woodard, and Kummer, 2014, 319), is ignored.

Accountability: Learning Turned Upside Down

Choices in traditional public education about teaching, learning, and achievement under these circumstances have been converted from a universe of academic discourse to the tiny island of *accountability to* the free market (Swensson and Shaffer, 2020; Tichnor-Wagner, Harrison, and Cohen-Vogel, 2016).

Accountability to imposed in the form of standardized testing alters the activities natural to public education.

Teaching, for example, is relegated to *test prep* (Barnum, 2018b). Learning is rationed. For students whose standardized test scores are just below the passing or "cut" score, extra time and opportunity for learning is maximized to "push" scores above the cut score.

As Hursh (2007) points out, the frenzy to increase the number of students who pass tests is nothing less than "educational triage [that] exacerbates educational inequality as the students who either pass or are close to passing the test become valued commodities and those students who need the most help are left to fend for themselves" (507).

Accountability to: "Failure" for Educational Control

Accountability to is heralded as the means necessary to force public education to measure up to expectations linked to free market theory (Au, 2010; Barnum, 2018a; Garza and Garza, 2010).

As Stitzlein (2015) points out, "accountability is a term that is often used when there is a problem and someone or some institution serving the public must give an account for failing to meet expectations of the public" (572).

An emphasis on failure assigned to traditional public education in terms of accountability to free market theory is integral to is control of US schooling (Au, 2010). Test results are false clues that lead teaching and learning astray because free market theory expects that learning and US history are fixed things, "a single master narrative" (Silverstein, 2021).

Accountability to forces traditional public education to define students, learning, and teaching in adult-centric terms. *Accountability to* thereby becomes the primary instrument utilized to generate a consumer relations frenzy for marketplace education. Control is leveraged across teaching and learning in free market intentions masquerading as reform.

Free market schemes embedded in *accountability to* ensure that America's public education is out of balance, tilted toward expectations that fulfill the principles of an ideology.

These principles, taken for granted by proponents of marketplace schooling, establish standardized testing and the tenets of free market theory as nonnegotiables for education without engaging in an obvious question: *What is accountability?*

THREE'S A CROWD: THE DEFINITIONS
OF ACCOUNTABILITY

Key terms in US education often have multiple formal definitions. Accountability is no exception. Two of these definitions are identified by Elmore (2005):

- *External Accountability:* External accountability is the imposition of requirements for education by statute, rule, or mandate.* Authorities with a statutory or regulatory interest in traditional public education impose external accountability.

    (*Author's note: US public education, properly, is connected to regulations, statutes, and mandates generated by state and federal government that administer, among other things, expectations about school safety, student health, and/or democratic values. However, external accountability can impose ideological expectations for school performance. Many of these expectations are devoid of a focus on growing student intelligence and resort to reform and control on behalf of adult-centric intentions.)
- *Internal Accountability:* "The alignment of individual values with collective expectations, reinforced by the processes of accountability, results in internal accountability" (Elmore, 2005, 135–36).

Hors d'oeuvres: Accountability on the Side

Relegated on the menu of public education to the equivalent of an hors d'oeuvre, a third definition of accountability suggests the potential impact of public connections on behalf of equity in US education:

- *Responsible Accountability:* This iteration of accountability envisions public education, unto itself, "as public accountability (particularly from lawmakers) for equitable educational opportunities, attention to varied educational purposes, [and] a greater role for professional judgment in assessment of educational quality" (Gunzenhauser and Hyde, 2007, 495–96).

Accountability and its Assumptions

Several assumptions exist in these definitions and dictate a free market tendency throughout contemporary notions of accountability.

For instance, both external and internal accountability incorporate the assumption that accountability is most effective when it is imposed from a source external to an entity, in this case, traditional public education.

Another assumption is that educators, despite extensive experience with assessment, (1) are incapable of taking responsibility for meeting expectations and (2) that accountability must be mandated to correct this problem.

The impact of these assumptions and the means utilized to act upon them (e.g., standardized testing) "reduce[s] local discretion, autonomy and creativity, narrow[s] curriculum; and constrain[s] teaching pedagogy (Toenjes, Dworking, Gary, Jon, and Antwanett, 2000)" (Goldring and Greenfield, 2002, 10).

Alive and well in these assumptions is that accountability is necessary because traditional public educators are untrustworthy and/or inept. Accountability to is disdain for the exercise of professional judgment about student learning in the classroom (Reimers, 2006).

Accountability to: Distortion and Control

In place of professional judgment and assessment in public school classrooms implemented in pursuit of student-centric intentions, *accountability to* intervenes in education in pursuit of the certainty expected from adult-centric intentions.

"The fog of certainty forces educators to devote 'inordinate time [to] concern about students' scores and not enough to students' learning' (Gunzenhauser, 2003, p. 56)" (Swensson and Shaffer, 2020, 61). Insinuations about learning drawn from standardized test data ensure certainty represented by learning as a fixed state and by marketplace comfort zones.

The assumption at the foundation of the definition of responsible accountability is that *public accountability* is a substantive effort made by all state legislatures.

Ample scholarship indicates that this is a false assumption (Baker, DiCarlo, and Weber, 2019; Darling-Hammond, 2019). Public accountability, it turns out, is jettisoned by numerous state legislatures. In its place, educational gerrymandering, funding shortfalls, and ALEC-infused statutes represent the deleterious impact on public education of *accountability to*.

CHOOSING THE FUTURE: DID YOU WANT ACCOUNTABILITY WITH THAT?

Accountability to vs. *accountability for* is an arbiter of choice with which public educators can differentiate among the intentions of each major perspective about education (Swensson, Lehman, and Ellis, 2021). In part, the struggle over primary purpose for the future of America's education is a clash over separate accountabilities.

The struggle over choice, in this case, is complicated by the status of *accountability to.* If public educators were using a menu to select between these versions of accountability, one version would be the only, obligatory, entrée: *accountability to.*

Missing entirely from this menu is *accountability for all students.* *Accountability for* is professional judgment applied by public educators to determine the extent of student learning and, using this judgment, reflect and act to improve student intelligence.

Accountability to **Free Market Theory**

Accountability to free market theory justifies the worth of US education by the extent that schools manifest the forms prioritized by free market theory.

Accountability to is the expectation that adult-centric intentions suffuse teaching and learning. *Accountability to*, as a result, is the commitment by proponents of privatization education to forms such as efficiency, educational choice, and singularity.

Accountability to: **The Form of Efficiency**

Assertions about the value of efficiency are bulwarks of *accountability to*:

- "The value of efficiency in a free market [is] among the central concepts within their agenda: less government, preservation of individual wealth, and ideological purity" (Swensson, Ellis, and Shaffer, 2019a, 94).
- Fiscal efficiency is attained by denying enrollment in privatization schools to expensive students (e.g., special needs, English Language Learners) (Swensson, Ellis, and Shaffer, 2019b).
- Mechanisms and privatization schools that retain or increase enrollment, especially when enrollment growth occurs because students left other schools, are efficient (Murray and Howe, 2017; Swensson, Ellis, and Shaffer, 2019a). Evidence of inefficiency is demonstrated when schools are abandoned by parents/caregivers and their students.

Accountability to free market theory "is largely an economic concern, where taxpayers seek efficient use of their money and a satisfying rate of return on their investment in children" (Stitzlein, 2015, 564). Efficiency is a tenet of free market theory and valued in US education for its correspondence with operating like a private sector business (Anderson and Donchik, 2016).

Accountability to: The Form of Educational Choice

Educational choice is a form natural to privatization education. Educational choice is predefined as socially valuable when it "'denies the importance of public goods or else maintains that all our goods are best achieved by individuals acting out of individual self-interest'" (Hostetler, 2003, 355).

Accountability to embraces a double paradox: educational choice not only prioritizes singularity but also identifies public goods as individual goods.

This paradox explains, in part, how choice enables limitation and restriction to generate profit within privatization schools. "Profit can be squeezed out of pure implementation of free market schooling because 'private voucher schools can discriminate against students based on their religion, LGBT status, disability, academic achievement, and disciplinary history' (Weaver, 2018, para. 10)" (Swensson, Lehman, and Ellis, 2021, 98).

Accountability to: The Form of Singularity

Singularity is a socially valuable form of privatization education that encourages denial of enrollment by predetermined student cohorts. "Singularity (thinking and acting exclusively on behalf of the self-aggrandizement of individuals or socially valuable cohorts) excludes 'the other'" (Swensson and Lehman, 2021, 98).

Singularity and profit commingle because choice schools often locate in neighborhoods or areas where families already pay the cost of privatization schooling or locate in states where vouchers and/or tax credits are funding sources available to students who already attend free market schools (Gilblom and Sang, 2019).

SOLD IN THE MARKETPLACE

An ample supply of adult-centric intentions is available to shoppers in the educational marketplace. *Accountability to* facilitates the sale of intentions and activities natural to privatization education:

- *Competition:* Free market theory intends that competition among schools will force inefficient schools to fall by the wayside when families leave to choose surviving, efficient, schools (Chubb and Moe, 1990; Barrow and Rouse, 2008; Loeb, Valant, and Kasman, 2011, 141). *Accountability to* operationalizes this winner-take-all scenario because "competition can encourage 'isomorphism,' or standardization, to a single model" (Lubienski, Gulosino, and Weitzel, 2009, 608). Competition based on the choice and efficiency produced by standardized test scores gives *accountability to* a "certainty advantage" whereby parents and caregivers "remove their children from schools receiving low grades [which] will ultimately ensure that only high-performing schools survive" (Murray and Howe, 2017, 4).

- *Preferred Customers: Accountability to* justifies reflection and action that seeks out and serves preferred customers in the marketplace. For instance, in Indiana more than "90 percent of voucher schools are considered to be religiously affiliated (IDOE, 2014c)" (Cierniak, Billick, and Ruddy, 2015, 9). Parents and caregivers respond to this form when, "in districts that participate in choice, white and more affluent parents have fled as poorer, minority kids have come into their schools, exacerbating de facto segregation" (Strauss, 2016). Privatization education doubles-down on this phenomenon via enrollment processes that "accept or deny applicants as they see fit" (Petrilli, M., Finn, C., Hentges, C., and Northern, A. M., 2009, 9). As intentions central to free market theory, self-aggrandizement, and singularity are offered to preferred customers via *accountability to.*

ACCOUNTABILITY TO THE ECONOMIC MAN

At the forefront of adult-centric intentions is economic supremacy. *Accountability to* "equates the political man with the economic man, arguing that policymakers create laws as if they were competitors in an open market, choosing options that preserve their status over those which generate the most public good (Kelman, 1987)" (Dawkins-Law, 2014, 2).

Equating self-aggrandizement with the public good is carte blanche for free market proponents to make "the regular suggestion that students are in school primarily to acquire marketable skills to be cashed in for employment" (Strike, 2008, 121).

Despite the mythical calculations that undergird this notion of reform in US public education, "private interests oriented toward education as a vehicle for both individual and national economic gain shaped 'reform' documents of the 1980s and 1990s" (Knight Abowitz, 2008, 362).

Accountability to weds this myopic intention to a contemporary narrative about US education that fails to account for the inevitability that today's marketable skills are not necessarily the marketable skills of tomorrow. This retrograde emphasis on the economic man precludes a robust roster of subject area offerings for all students in public schools. The implementation of *accountability to* denies students a broad spectrum of potential life successes.

Measuring *Accountability to*

Standardized testing is the nationwide phenomenon that measures the degree to which traditional public schools are accountable *to* free market theory. Standardized measurement is employed to sanction traditional public education and enforce the imposition of *accountability to*.

Enforcing marketplace expectations with the cudgel of test scores ensures that a tautology emerges when *accountability to* operates in accordance with a "basic logic of the system, which is that the thing that will drive school improvement is pushing people to improve test scores" (Barnum, 2018b; Garza and Garza, 2010).

The corrosive impact of this reasoning is that standardized testing infiltrates practice throughout traditional public education. Control over day-to-day practice is exercised when annual state testing data mandates judgment about a school's efficiency. Test metrics accelerate "the introduction of performance-based accountability—policies that evaluate, reward, and sanction schools on the basis of measured performance" (Elmore, 2005, 134).

Performance measures inflict a wide range of what will be referred to in this discussion as *uncritical habits of mind* across the landscape of US education within decisions that control schooling. Policies, statutes, and expectations that arise with *accountability to* apply

> pressures [that] influence what teachers teach, marginalize low-stakes subjects, divert resources to students based on their likelihood of passing the test, and increase the time devoted to teaching test taking skills as distinct from the content being tested (Booher-Jennings, 2006; Diamond & Spillane, 2004; Firestone, Mayrowetz, and Fairman, 1998; Jacob, 2005; McNeil, 2002; Smith, 1998; Valenzuela, 2004; Wilson and Floden, 2001). (Spillane, Parise, and Zoltners Sherer, 2011, 586–87)

MEASURED PERFORMANCE, LEARNING FORSAKEN

Measured performance via standardized tests abandons student intelligence when:

1. The lower-order cognition embedded in standardized tests do "students a disservice, as these kinds of exams are less likely to foster thinking

critically and applying knowledge and further do not appear to even promote acquisition and retention of factual information to the extent stimulated by higher-order exams" (Jensen, McDaniel, Woodard, and Kummer, 2014, 319).

2. In response to requirements and penalties associated with standardized testing, educators revert to classroom instruction known as *test prep* (Barnum, 2018b) "This reactive instruction is a self-defense tactic that prepares students for 'predictable patterns in the test' (Barnum, 2018a)" (Swensson and Shaffer, 2020, 57).

3. Restrictions on teaching and learning imposed by standardized testing ensure that "children with creative and practical abilities, who are almost never taught or assessed in a way that matches their pattern of abilities, may be at a disadvantage in course after course, year after year" (Sternberg and Grigorenko, 2004, 278).

4. Standardized tests drive federal legislation (e.g., NCLB; ESSA), determine state-generated expectations, and "operate as a form of control over classroom practices and learning" (Au, 2010, 2).

The significance of certainty enforced by performance measures is that "learning outcomes, may be pursued because they are measureable and not because they are educative" (Webster, 2017, 332). Students are abandoned when learning is forsaken in lieu of *accountability to* tenets of free market theory.

Testing: Enforcing the Limitations of *Accountability to*

Hemmed in when free market tenets are prioritized, traditional public educators have little choice but to focus on instruction devoted to subjects included on standardized tests. The limits placed on teaching and learning in traditional public education grow from the characteristics of standardized tests:

1. standardized tests are time-limited to ensure that they measure test-taking skills, rote-learning, and intellectual efficiency;

2. standardized tests include a small number of questions about each tested standard which means that one or two incorrect responses can deflate a student's test results;

3. a "passing score" on a standardized test is different every year and this score is altered annually before tests are given. Educators are given no information in advance about either the score needed to pass or the overall learning standards singled out for testing;

4. cost reduction, facilitated when standardized tests are given online, ensures that standardized tests measure students' abilities to manipulate a computer and/or survive the glitches associated with online testing;
5. criteria used to establish passing scores and assign meaning to test results are little more than statistical gimmicks often justified by outright mumbo jumbo. Murray and Howe (2017) confirm that test results emerge from an overall process in which "the selection and weighting of criteria seem to have no basis other than the seat-of-the-pants intuitions of policymakers woefully lacking in technical knowledge and skills" (7).

Accountability to facilitates the abandonment of authentic learning and cognitive exploration in public education classrooms. The notion of choice ballyhooed by proponents of privatization education is nothing more than choice among the intentions of free market theory. Restricting choice to concepts and mechanisms exclusive to privatization education ensures that *accountability to* is an arbiter of choice for ideological purity.

The tenets of free market theory are a foundation for "schooling intended to benefit external entities, ideologically aligned adults, and a low-cost fiscal bottom line with only secondary regard for students" (Swensson, Lehman, and Ellis, 2021, 56). *Accountability to* free market theory represents the control achieved when adult-centric intentions predominate in US public education.

The Costs of Measured Performance

Although free market education adherents emphasize that investment in public education is a burden and that low-cost education should be prioritized, significant costs are associated with standardization of *accountability to*, including:

- The fifty states (in 2019) spend $1.7 billion annually on standardized testing (Penn State Sites, 2019).
- As exorbitant as this price is, the cost of testing is not only a matter of dollars and cents. As Stitzlein (2015) relates, disconnection from learning is a cost paid by teachers, learners, and schools because "accountability tends to be assigned or sought after the fact, once an action is completed" (573).

When standardized tests are administered in the spring, results are not available until the next fall. Not only does data from spring testing cause educators to return instruction to standards from the previous school year but test prep backpedals teaching and learning to lower-order cognition. Measured performance is a significant cost to learning and, ironically, when teaching backpedals, learning that would help students on the standardized test in the new school year is stymied.

- "Research indicates that test results—the numbers that signify account- ability and judgment about the quality of education and schools—have little positive effect (Patrick and Mantzicopoulos, 2016) on any aspect of public education" (Swensson and Shaffer, 2020, 58).

Accountability for **All Students**

Accountability for all students is the choice to engage learners with *how to think,* the moral obligation of public education, and the capacities required to balance individual and public goods (Swensson and Shaffer, 2020). Assessment measures the extent to which student-centric intentions are taught and learned in the educational environments fostered by *accountability for.*

Assessment of educational function in these environments and its effect on student learning look for "wise thinking [that] involves the ability to use one's intelligence in the service of a common good by balancing one's own interests with those of other people and of a broader community over both the short- and long-term" (Sternberg, Reznitskaya, and Jarvin, 2007, 150).

Accountability for invokes assessment as the best professional judgment of public educators about effective classroom engagement of all students with cognitive agency, successful intelligence, and wisdom:

- *Cognitive agency:* "Cognitive agency is the capacity to choose and act to balance behaviors that benefit both the good of the individual and the public good" (Swensson, Ellis, and Shaffer, 2019a, 84).
- *Successful intelligence:* "Successful intelligence is the use of an inte- grated set of abilities needed to attain success in life, however an individ- ual defines it, within his or her sociocultural context." . . . "Successfully intelligent people adapt to, shape and select environments" (Sternberg and Grigorenko, 2004, 274).
- *Wisdom:* Sternberg, Reznitskaya, and Jarvin (2007) define wisdom as:

  The application of intelligence, creativity, and knowledge as mediated by values toward the achievement of a common good through a *balance* among (a) intrapersonal, (b) interpersonal, and (c) extrapersonal interests, over the (a) short- and (b) long-terms, in order to achieve a balance among (a) adapta- tion to existing environments, (b) shaping of existing environments, and (c) selection of new environments (emphasis original). (145)

Happy Birthday, *Accountability for*

Accountability for all students turns two hundred years old near the middle of the twenty-first century. Horace Mann's (1839) pronouncement that enlightenment was the goal of the first public schools anchored *accountability for* all students at the center of US education.

Accountability for is enacted when learnable moments are identified so that public schools are "places where children learn how to express their ideas and respond to the ideas of others as they balance their own individual needs with collective needs" (Stitzlein, 2015, 567). *Accountability for* is a before-the-fact focus on educational function guided by instrumental agency to meet the learning needs of all students.

The positive student-centric effect of *accountability for* is suggested by Gallup Poll data from 2021, which reports that almost three-quarters of parents/caregivers with school-aged children were satisfied with the quality of their public schools (Grose, 2022).

Back to the Future: Assessment

Assessment is the multilayered and persistent process that public educators use to hold themselves accountable *for* student learning and the common good. Assessment is professional meaning-making about student learning.

Assessment is a public educator's wherewithal to improve learning and grow the meaning-making (e.g., cognitive, creative, and practical capabilities) of each student. Aided by a growing body of research about dynamic instruction, assessment means educators are accountable *for* student learning and the common good.

Assessment is substantively different from "achievement as measured solely by test scores" (Gunzenhauser and Hyde, 2007, 495). Assessment prioritizes learning as a whole that is more than the sum of its parts by "valuing *educational* concerns which may or may not lend themselves to measurement—such as thinking and being moral" (Webster, 2017, 333).

Teacher-designed assessments—both formative and summative—create daily opportunities to monitor and adjust instruction based on student learning. Assessment focuses professional responses on student progress. Assessment of learning allows public educators to hold themselves *accountable for* student learning and improved professional practice.

Accountability to and *accountability for* constitute one of the four duos with which educators can gather insights about the intentions of the major perspectives about US education. An arbiter of choice, accountability, one way or the other, is fundamental to the future of public education in America.

Chapter 5

Arbiters of Choice

Responsibility Given vs. Responsibility Accepted

EMAIL
To: Traditional Public Educators
Fr: Your Kindergarten Colleagues
Re: Our Responsibility

Public educators are confronted by responsibility as an arbiter of choice: either *given* or *accepted.*

Educators are given responsibility for socially valuable things identified by the tenets of free market theory.

Responsibility *given* to US educators, as Merritt, Kennedy, and Farnworth (2020) indicate, is a *commitment to consumer relations.* This commitment evokes the responsibilities assumed when an emperor in a folktale paraded about.

Responsibility to consumer relations facilitates ideological outreach to parents/caregivers who are both preferred and vulnerable customers in the eyes of proponents of free market schooling.

Accepting responsibility, on the other hand, is a commitment to the *public responsibility for education* (Merritt, Kennedy, and Farnworth, 2020). Educators accept responsibility for something greater than themselves: learning and the common good for all students.

The implications of responsibility given and responsibility accepted for the future purpose of public education are examined in the next chapter.

Toeing the line of free market theory is a responsibility given to enact adult-centric priorities. Commodification, competition, and self-aggrandizement—all emerge as consequences when responsibility to the marketplace is given to educators.

The outcome of responsibility given to America's schooling is *productivity.* Productivity is the epitome of *high minimum quality.* High minimum quality—the contemporary oxymoron that defines adequacy for public education—is guaranteed when education is expected to yield ROI (return on investment).

Accepting responsibility is a commitment to RTS (return to students). RTS develops when reflection and action yield instrumental agency necessary and sufficient to choose instruction designed to engage all students with authentic learning.

As an arbiter of choice, responsibility is given but not for learning or responsibility is accepted for the complexities of *how to think* on behalf of the common good.

SEPARATE RESPONSIBILITIES, DIFFERENT COMMITMENTS

Responsibility can be defined as a duty to deal with something or as having control over something or someone.

Responsibility for America's education is either *given* or *accepted.* The distinction between *accepting* responsibility and being *given* responsibility begins when an educator either

1. Accepts responsibility for something greater than self, or
2. Is given responsibility that succumbs to the "option of simply adopting activities which have been separated from their primary purposes and which others assume we ought to adopt" (Webster, 2017, 32).

Fundamentally different commitments are made when given, or accepting, responsibility. Merritt, Kennedy, and Farnworth (2020) differentiate these commitments as either accepting *public responsibility for education* or being given *responsibility for consumer relations.*

Public Responsibility for Education

Public responsibility for education is acceptance of the "unique responsibility to transmit an understanding of public values (e.g., equity, the common good, protection of individual rights) to the next generation of policymakers; public servants, residents; and citizens (Gould, 2011)" (Merritt, Kennedy, and Farnworth, 2020, 156).

Accepting public responsibility for education entails public value creation essential for teaching and learning in a democracy. Accepting public responsibility is a focus on students as democracy's future-public whose responsibility, in turn, will be to accept responsibility for the common good (Stitzlein, 2015).

Accepting public responsibility for education is a commitment to create learning environments where the intersection of *how to think* and the moral obligation of education engages learners with capacities for assuming personal cost for the common good.

For example, history suggests that social justice, the moral purpose necessary to address and eliminate marginalization in US education (Furman, 2012), is a responsibility accepted but rarely given.

Accepting responsibility, public educators commit to an a priori purpose or function for teaching and learning that entails "clear expectations for students' capabilities, what forms of knowledge are important for them to obtain, and how to assess students' progress toward achieving their educational aims" (Gunzenhauser and Hyde, 2007, 494).

Responsibility for Consumer Relations

When given responsibility for consumer relations, educators are duty-bound to deliver "educational services to students (and their parents, all as consumers) in a competitive marketplace" (Gunzenhauser and Hyde, 2007, 494).

In the marketplace, educators are given responsibility for socially valuable things aligned with the tenets of free market theory. Responsibility for consumer relations is given to educators to influence "vulnerable consumers [who] fail to understand their own preferences and/or lack the knowledge, skills, or freedom (i.e., personal prerogatives and marketplace options) to act on them" (Ringold, 2005, 202).

The barrage of consumer relations for educational reform through adherence to free market education and adult-centric intentions has had an impact. "'The public has been persuaded that significant sectors of public education are underperforming and that solving this problem is more a matter of mobilizing will and competence than providing additional resources or new knowledge'" (Knight Abowitz, 2008, 363).

*The Educational Marketplace at Work: Vulnerable,
then, Invulnerable*

Given responsibility for consumer relations, proponents of privatization education manipulate and persuade individuals perceived as vulnerable to "shop" in the privatization marketplace. Consumers are fed a steady diet of self-aggrandizing designs and promises aligned with adult-centric intentions.

A responsibility for consumer relations, moreover, justifies ideological blandishments that reassure preferred customers that they are *invulnerable* if wrapped in the ideological arms of singularity—one of many marketplace comfort zones—provided in privatization education.

Responsibility for consumer relations not only promotes the commercialization of US education, but also gives legislators, state authorities, and ideologues justification to create mandates for the acquisitive practices of marketplace principles in privatization schools and for the profit motive of charter management companies (Figlio and Hart, 2010; Zernike, 2016).

Under these circumstances, public educators and public schools are subject to statutes, processes, and regulations that require a commitment to "'compliance without competence'" (Gunzenhauser and Hyde, 2007, 502). Marketplace incompetence is an obvious feature of the student-centric intentions of traditional public education that free market proponents leverage with sanctions and measured performance to impose compliance.

An Educator's Choice about Responsibility

Accepting public responsibility for ends greater than self is an educator's commitment to "responsibility [that] resides in personal action that one *should take*, though it can be individual or collective" (emphasis added) (Stitzlein, 2015, 572). Public educators accept responsibility for influencing the learning and future of every student.

When *given* responsibility to consumer relations, however, educators commit to meeting expectations aligned with the tenets of free market theory. When given responsibility, educators revert to function follows form. Given responsibility to consumer relations, educators are subject to forms and means from which schooling cannot deviate.

RESPONSIBILITY GIVEN: PARADING IN ROYAL CLOTHING

Given responsibility for consumer relations on behalf of adult-centric intentions, choices made by marketeers about education evoke a comparison with a folktale about an emperor on parade. Given responsibility for consumer relations, like the emperor on parade, marketeers wear very little related to learning.

A Splendid Cloak: Education as a Commodity

In the world of commerce, a commodity is a primary agricultural product or raw material. Sugar, copper, and pork bellies, are among the commodities that lend themselves to speculative business practices.

As it is envisioned by free market proponents, US public education is a commodity (Lee, 2018). Just like pork bellies, privatization education is manipulated by speculative practices that seek a return from cost reduction, profit maximization, and risk management (Swensson, Lehman, and Ellis, 2021). Under the aegis of free market thinking, public education is bought and sold to maximize ROI in the forms of ideological purity and monetary profit.

Marketeers, the proponents of free market education (Swensson, Ellis, and Shaffer, 2019a), buy and sell in bulk (e.g., charter schools, virtual education, vouchers) to attain both purity and profit. The commodification of education gives marketeers responsibilities to:

- *Protect market share*: "Charter schools in competitive markets protect their market position by opting for less costly and more easily educated students, and by excluding students from low-income or single-parent families" (Lee, 2018, 13).
- *Avoid product spoilage*: "Private voucher schools can discriminate against students based on their religion, LGBT status, disability, academic achievement, and disciplinary history" (Weaver, 2018, para. 10). Privatization schools "can be segregated by academic ability and disability, ethnicity, economics, language, and culture" (Underwood and Mead, 2012, 5). Free market enrollment practices "generally favor allowing participating schools to accept or deny applicants as they see fit" (Finn, Hentges, Petrilli, and Winkler, 2009, 9).
- *Buy low. Sell high*: "Buy low and sell high" is a free market mantra. For example, this phrase is tailor-made for the responsibility given to businesses who offer virtual schools (e.g., K-12 Inc., Connections Academy). Online schooling is where negligible overhead and large student/teacher ratios ensure that "some of the largest cyber charter companies are bringing in multi-million-dollar annual revenue streams" (Elder, 2014).
- *Sell "the sizzle"*: In the marketplace, "sizzle" sells. "Selling 'sizzle' in the market for privatization education involves the satisfying 'pop' of ideology (e.g., choice, parent rights, productivity), the 'crackle' of the come-on of preference substitution (e.g., sectarian education, restricted enrollment, distance learning), and/or the siren song of self-aggrandizement" (e.g., profit, *accountability to*).

Like any other aspect of responsibility given to free market adherents, commodification is a game where winners and losers are expected and encouraged.

Worthy Pantaloons: Education as a Competition

Free market theory and privatization education wallow in competition (Lubienski, Gulosino, and Weitzel, 2009).

Survival of the fittest and a dog-eat-dog marketplace are responsibilities given to privatization education adherents to challenge, and cure, the maladies that afflict traditional US public education (DeAngelis and Erickson, 2018).

For proponents of privatization education, winning and losing are inevitable because "no one has a strong incentive to make sure that the public good is well provided" (Shaw, 2010, 242). The responsibility given to those who favor competition between schools is a commitment to avoid the public good.

Lee (2018) describes this as the calamity of responsibility-given whereby "processes of privatization in education and commodification of schooling fundamentally challenge the two conditions of non-excludability and non-rivalrousness essential to define a public good (Labaree, 1997; Lubienski, 2006)" (14).

Marketplace proponents are given responsibility for rivalrous and exclusionary education. In the marketplace for American schooling, competition begets excellence in the form of "winning" schools (Swensson and Shaffer, 2020). But, competition means that "loser" schools and "loser" students are inevitable.

Free market education adherents blithely portray losing as an expectation and benefit of competition (Swensson, Ellis, and Shaffer, 2019a). Buying and selling commodities, after all, is a risky business.

"Efficiency is defined as the culling of inefficient schools when these schools are abandoned by parents and caregivers with the result that fiscal support supplied by mechanisms is withdrawn" (Swensson, Ellis, and Shaffer, 2019a, 11). Students and parents/caregivers who play the game of marketplace education have little recourse if their existence as an educational commodity becomes a losing proposition.

A Magnificent Hat: Education Owes Me

Responsibility given to educators demands a Return on Investment (ROI). ROI turns the tables on the old-fashioned idea of an IOU ("I owe you").

Instead of public education "owing" learning and the common good to students and society, marketeers employ free market theory to create education that, for them, is a UO-me ("You owe me"). In other words, US education doesn't owe students or society anything; it owes a return to marketeers.

From the perspective of marketeers, a return is owed to citizens and corporations whose taxes pay the costs of US public education (Stitzlein, 2015). ROI is nothing less than the adult-centric intention that public education owes a fiduciary and/or ideological return to every "me" who supports free market theory or who suffers the burden of public education as a cost. The responsibility given to marketeers is a commitment to economic instead of educational returns.

ANSWERS TO A MARKETEER'S QUESTION

The "R" in ROI promises an answer to every marketeer's essential question about public education: *What's in this for me?* Answers to this question reveal the blue-chip returns intended when free market theory is coupled with US education:

- Imbue students with core ideas of free market theory. "Students are taught to see themselves as being in competition with others for scarce opportunities and goods" (Strike, 2008, 121).
- Turn a blind eye to improving student achievement. Studies reveal that most privatization education produces achievement returns for students that are inferior or equal to academic levels attained in traditional US public education (Abdulkadiroglu, Pathak, and Walters, 2015; Brown, 2017; DeBray-Pelot, Lubienski, and Scott, 2007; Cowen, Fleming, Witte, and Wolf, 2012; Figlio and Hart, 2010; Loeb, Valane, and Kasman, 2011; Lubienski, 2013; Rouse and Barrow, 2008; Sass, Zimmer, Gill, and Booker, 2016).
- Embrace adult-centric intentions. "Instead of equity for students, equity for taxpayers is often the baseline for school funding (Knoeppel, Pitts, and Lindle, 2013)" (Swensson, Lehman, and Ellis, 2021, 125–26). In combination, competition, standardized testing, and inequity emerge in an educational marketplace where responsibility accepted for RTS (Return to Students) is rejected (Swensson, Ellis, and Shaffer, 2019a).
- Take responsibility for neither the common good nor citizenship in a democracy. Nearly 75 percent of US voucher schools are religious (Klein, 2017, 4); approximately 50 percent of the nation's students who attend charter schools are enrolled in an institution that is corporation-managed (Stitzlein, 2017); and more than 80 percent of America's students who attend a private school are educated in schools operated by a religious organization (Kaufman, 2017; Smith, 2017).

- Maximize insufficient funding to fulfill the low-cost imperatives of free market theory. Thirty-two of the fifty states provide flat or regressive funding distribution to public education (Farrie et al., 2019). Baker, DiCarlo, and Weber (2019) find that "the fact that so many states are either non-progressive or regressive is *by design*" (emphasis original) (19).
- Maximize responsibility for consumer relations to hype the competitive advantages of markets and promote the ideological axiom that free markets distribute resources with greater efficiency than any bureaucratic monopoly, like traditional public education, ever could (Hess, 2010; Rouse and Barrow, 2008).

Given responsibility for public relations to enact adult-centric intentions, proponents of free market theory transform the hunt for educational purpose into a zero-sum game. Under these rules, competition and commodification deliver a winning return to adults while students lose. The responsibility given to marketeers, ideologues, and other adherents of free market theory promotes control of public schooling so that returns to students are a secondary consideration.

HOW TO MAXIMIZE THE "R" IN ROI? PRODUCTIVITY!

Productivity is a marketplace responsibility. Free market schools are celebrated for productivity "either because they produce higher student gains at a lower cost or because they produce similar or only slightly lower student outcomes at a significantly lower cost" (Wolf et al., 2014, 8). Productivity is the epitome of high minimum quality.

Productivity is in sync with the bottom line for any marketplace. "Maximum output and efficiency by an organization can best be accomplished if there is an opportunity to make a profit; and we should encourage private vendors to enter public education with the profit motive in mind to increase productivity" (Brown, 2002, 250). Productivity is facilitated by cost effectiveness and ROI (Wolf et al., 2014).

The path taken by privatization education advocates is littered with learnable moments similar to those envisioned by the Milwaukee Parental Choice Program (MPCP) which "was designed to increase productivity [compared to traditional public schools] by obtaining similar or increased educational outcomes for students for substantially less taxpayer support" (Ford, 2016, 883).

PRODUCTIVITY: WHEN THE "R" IN ROI IS FOR *RISK*

Given responsibility for productivity, free market proponents ignore the risk of irresponsibility in adult-centric intentions for the educational marketplace.

For instance, in Michigan, where 80 percent of charter schools are operated by for-profit management companies, productivity unleashes bounteous fiscal irresponsibility "including waste, fraud and abuse, lack of accountability over federal funds and lack of assurances that the schools were implementing federal programs in accordance with federal requirements" (Gorman, 2016).

In addition, despite consumer relations hype about the free market, even proponents of vouchers are unable to verify that "productive efficiency is maximized when schools produce a given level and type of education for the least cost" (Belfield and Levin, 2005, 554).

Marching to the rhythm of productivity, free market proponents stay in step with marketplace Muzak. Several popular tunes provide the backbeat for productivity:

- *Tune #1—You Ain't Nothin' but Minimum Quality*: Adequacy in traditional US public education has been commandeered by legal theory and is defined as *high minimum quality* (Umpstead, 2007). This prevailing notion about adequacy ensures that responsibility given to educators can be labeled productive when it evinces efficiency at low cost. Educational adequacy, in this instance, is "a level of resources or inputs that is sufficient to meet defined or absolute, rather than relative, output standards, such as a minimum passing score on a state achievement test" (Umpstead, 2007, 282).

  Understanding adequacy in this way gives carte blanche to legislators and state authorities to establish public education that is nothing more than "a measure of whether the amount of funding for schools is enough for students to reach a minimal level of educational outcomes" (Baker, DiCarlo, and Weber, 2019, 9). One of the least tenable assumptions built into this definition of adequacy is that learning is linear (Ilgen, Hollenbeck, Johnson, and Jundt, 2005).

  Invoking educational adequacy as a minimum supports the propensity of legislatures to gerrymander state funding to promote low cost (Black, 2019). When minimums suffice for adequacy in public education, preference substitution as intentional underfunding is justified. Adequacy aligned with adult-centric intentions is given credit for establishing productivity while no responsibility is taken for shortchanging students (Swensson, Lehman, and Ellis, 2021).

- *"B-Side" Tune 2: Minimum Productivity USA:* Adequacy as a minimum means that *the public* is given responsibility to cope with low-cost productivity fostered by educational gerrymandering. Because commodification of education justifies buy-low minimums, legislatures have few qualms about foisting upon individual school districts a portion of school funding without determining if the tax base in a district has the capacity to ante up the remainder of the state's portion of the funding (Black, 2019).

  Although all school districts must dance to the tune of minimums for fiscal insufficiency, all school districts cannot respond with the same level of investment to compensate for shortfalls. Compensating for the minimums of productivity is subject to "local willingness to pay for public elementary and secondary education, differences in the costs of educating various categories of high-need pupils, or differences in the costs of providing education services in different geographic areas" (Skinner, 2019, 9).

  The melody line of "Minimum Productivity USA" is in harmony with adult-centric intentions when "the state engages in targeted partiality toward some students and denies other students the impartiality that equal protection demands" (Black, 2019, 1424).

  Targeted partiality in support of adequacy as a minimum is a feature of marketplace thinking that leaves students mired in day-to-day inadequacies including "uncertified teachers in classrooms, missing English-learner programs and the absence of basic services" (Sciarra and Hunter, 2015, 4).

  Some schools, communities, and/or individuals escape intentional inadequacy when privileges in the marketplace (e.g., wealth, race, political connections) deftly sidestep every minimum. Accepting minimums as adequacy for learning in a winner-take-all environment constitutes the moral irresponsibility of competition and educational gerrymandering foisted on innumerable public schools in the name of productivity.
- *Tune #3—Education Potion No. 9*: Wolf et al., (2014), describe productivity as a mystical potion brewed when ROI is calculated by the conversion of

  learning gains developed over time by students in the public charter and TPS [Traditional Public School] sectors into an estimate of the economic returns over a lifetime of students and comparing those returns to the revenue amounts invested in their education. (8)

  Productivity, thus, is calculated by imagining, supposing, and inventing the future earnings of students.

Concocting "learning gains" from minimum adequacy that "estimate" any student's lifetime "economic returns" lays bare the irresponsible fantasy of productivity. Reform in the shape of productivity promises the same level of accountability as the prognostications accessed from a Ouija board.

Productivity is nothing more than a "façade built out of numbers, speculation, and ideology, [that] represents low-cost teaching and learning sought through free market schooling" (Swensson, Lehman, and Ellis, 2021, 67).

- *Tune #4—Comfort Zones Around the Clock*: Teaching and learning are laden with uncertainties. Uncertainties are anathema to free market theory.

Productivity, low cost, and efficiency are bulwarks against risk. Rejecting uncertainties, policy makers and state authorities seek stability and ideological security offered by the tenets of free market theory. Arraying adult-centric intentions against uncertainties symbolized by the wasteful inefficiencies of RTS in public education, free market theory concocts privatization education as a comfort zone.

Free market comfort zones give responsibility to legislators, ideologues, and others to safeguard minimum adequacy with discrimination, restrictions tied to the weak definition of adequacy, inequitable resources, and/or unreliable leadership theories (Swensson and Shaffer, 2020; Swensson and Lehman, 2021).

IRRESPONSIBILITY: AVERSION SOLD HERE

Educational antipathy, stipulated in this discussion as aversion to student-centric intentions, is the primary irresponsibility of the marketplace. Choices made under the influence of educational antipathy about the future of US public education thwart "the capacity of a system to engage in the complexities of continuous improvement consistent with deep values of human purpose (Fullan, 2005, p. 114)" (Leo and Wickenberg, 2013, 407).

Educational antipathy takes educators and state authorities beyond mere dislike of traditional public education. Commodification, competition, and productivity are priorities in the marketplace for schooling that inject the narrative about the history for the future of US education with:

- Aversion to the uncertainties of teaching and learning alongside acceptance of productivity secured by comfort zones.
- Aversion to equity, employment of university-trained educators, and sufficient funding for public schools.

- Aversion to the capacity for learning in all students.
- Aversion to the common good as the role of America's public sector. Singularity and competition pave the road that leads to educational antipathy.
- Aversion to *the public* that excludes those individuals who do not "belong" in or "qualify" for privatization education.

Competing for the lowest cost, most efficient, and least regulated commodity, proponents of privatization education and its intentions justify rivalry and exclusion as means to assure the primacy of the individual in US education. Educational antipathy thrives on the assumption that adult-centric intentions facilitate efficiency and the belief that mechanisms define education (DeAngelis and Erickson, 2018; Shaw, 2010).

As it turns out, when given responsibility, what you see is what you get. Accepting responsibility entails ignoring the parade in the marketplace and turning toward the obligations inherent in a commitment to things greater than self.

Chapter 6

Arbiters of Choice

Burden vs. Obligation

EMAIL
To: Traditional Public Educators
Fr: The Electives Teachers
Re: Heavy Lifting in Our Profession

There is a natural human propensity "to detect familiar patterns and classify the world [which] can lock us into rigid patterns of action and trap us in the categories we invent (Langer, 1989)" (Ritchart and Perkins, 2005, 776). Free market theory represents the classification of the world and the rigid patterns of action for privatization into which ideologues, state authorities, legislators, and others have locked themselves.

This propensity drives efforts to eliminate heavy lifting associated with the obligations undertaken in traditional public education.

As the upcoming chapter reveals, obligations generally assumed as part of being a public educator (e.g., *learning*, *investment*, and *covenant*) are identified as inconvenient lessons, burdens perceived through the lens of free market theory.

Marketplace expectations dictate rigid patterns of action in pursuit of efficiency, low cost, and self-aggrandizement. Stasis, discrimination, and singularity are familiar free market patterns that lock-in free market theory and shed the burdens of traditional public schooling.

The upcoming chapter contrasts the *moral obligation* of traditional public education with the rigid *patterns of amorality* in free market education.

The purpose or function of moral obligation in public education is discussed as "the good." "The good" is an obligation to non-rivalrous and non-excludable intentions for public education (Lee, 2018).

As an end-in-mind, "the good" embraces moral obligation in public education which is expressed as "principles dealing with honesty, fairness, protection of the weak, and respect for all people (Clark, 1990, p. 252)" (Campbell, 2008, 602).

Moral obligation seeks *intradependence* and mutuality through which a stable democracy is achieved. Traditional public education is the historic mainspring sustaining citizenship aligned with this obligation. Free market education casts these obligations aside.

Moral obligation involves a choice of moral purpose fueled by each educator's self-mastery. This discussion examines the impact of interpretation on moral obligation. Interpretation and one of its consequences, *intentional impermanence*, suggest the challenges that confront a choice between the intentions of burden and obligation.

IS DUTY A HARDSHIP OR A MORAL COMMITMENT?

Burdens vs. *obligations* may be the most confusing of the arbiters of choice. Ironically, confusion mounts the further a discussion about obligation and burden proceeds.

At first, definitions are helpful. A burden is a duty that is a hardship or a nuisance. An obligation is a course of action to which a person is morally or legally committed.

To juxtapose a duty that is a hardship with a duty that is a moral or legal obligation seems, at least, nonsensical. But, educators must make sense out of this dichotomy because proponents of both perspectives have a duty.

The duty to enact student-centric intentions encompasses the flexible, uncertain, varied, and complex elements of teaching and learning. But, this duty is rejected when proponents of adult-centric intentions perceive the obligations of traditional public education as unnecessary hardships. If there is an obligation undertaken by marketeers, it is to rid US education of the burdens in traditional public schooling.

To Jettison Hardship, Invoke Rigid Patterns

Free market theory adherents are obliged to detect and align with familiar patterns and rigid beliefs (Ritchart and Perkins, 2005). Proponents of free market schooling, then, classify education as a limited, singular, competitive, self-aggrandizing enterprise. Locked in to this propensity, marketeers render the obligations of traditional public education as burdens.

ONE BURDEN THAT BINDS THEM ALL

Woven into the fabric of life, learning is a capacity that all human beings possess. Meaning-making and natural thinking are examples of this capacity.

Educere, the Latin root of the word education meaning to lead out, symbolizes the reflection and action involved teaching and learning (Swensson, Ellis, and Shaffer, 2019b). Formal learning experiences in traditional public education are *educere* in action.

Formal education experiences in public education represent a legal, moral, constitutional, and societal obligation to *lead out* meaning-making and natural thinking so that an individual's intelligence (i.e., analytic, creative, practical) grows and improves to benefit both individuals and the society in which they live.

Marketeers identify learning in traditional public education as a burden because these formal learning experiences run afoul of marketplace principles. Resorting to rigid patterns and the categories they invent, marketeers reject the intentions for *educere* because:

- *Learning is costly.* Not only are university-trained public educators paid via taxation to engage all students successfully with instruction but costly "extra" programs (e.g., special education services, elective classes, English Language Learning) aggravate the tax-supported cost of public education.
- *Learning often involves cognitive dissonance.* This state of cognitive uncertainty is an intolerable burden because it confounds productivity. Cognitive dissonance is the burden of uncertainty detrimental to comfort zones, stasis, and the inviolable patterns from which marketeers cannot deviate.
- *Learning is not necessarily a linear process.* Learning does not happen in a cognitive straight line. Moreover, learning is not always successful the first time. Too much time spent on these inefficiencies represents a burden that weighs down free market insistence on ROI from schooling.
- *Learning doesn't always align with* free market patterns or the proclivities of individual families. Learning is a burden, in the eyes of marketeers, when it dictates "increased uniformity of schools [which] reduce[s] parental options and the ability to match child-rearing preferences of parents to school experiences" (Levin, 2002, 161).

THE BURDEN CARRIED UPHILL
BOTH WAYS TO SCHOOL

America's taxpayers invest heavily in traditional public education. States and localities fund 92 percent of the investment in traditional US public education (Carey and Harris, 2016) and the nation's total investment in public schools is significant.

"From school year 2014–2015 to school year 2015–16, total revenue for public schools increased by $27 billion (4 percent), from $670 billion to $706 billion in constant 2017–18 dollars" (McFarland et al., 2019, 137). Total expenditures for 2017–18 (in constant 2019–20 dollars) "amounted to $762 billion" (National Center for Education Statistics, 2022).

Uphill to School

The burden carried uphill to school is the nation's investment in traditional public education. Free market theory adherents tender a number of ways to reduce this load:

- Gerrymandering educational funding across the fifty states (Black, 2019), promulgating a variety of tax-avoidance schemes, and installing free market mechanisms to redistribute and reduce investment. Reducing the burden of investment, proponents of privatization education celebrate the claim that privatization education costs less per student compared with traditional public education (Brown, 2017).
- Mechanisms (e.g., vouchers, tax credit scholarships) reduce the burden of investment by draining the public coffers of funding for traditional public schools. Reduced funding for public education coupled with state funding for privatization education means it becomes "less costly for parents to opt out of their residentially assigned public school in order to send their children to the school that better fits their needs" (DeAngelis and Erickson, 2018, 248).
- Disdain for investment in traditional public education advantages free market proponents in two ways. First, less funding for traditional schools fulfills the marketplace imperatives for less cost and less government. Second, less funding for traditional public education means less capacity to meet the learning needs of all students. Tossing aside the burden of investment gives the marketplace control over the destruction of its competition.

Uphill after School

The burden carried uphill away from school is equity. The burdens of educating all students and engaging fully with students whose needs require extra investment are problematic for true believers in free market theory.

In fact, both equity and equality are burdens that complicate the fulfillment of marketplace principles. Equity is a burden because learning is not linear in the sense that human beings learn at different rates. In addition, students with special needs, students whose first language is not English, and students in poverty require support for learning that other students do not.

Equality is a major burden for the marketplace. If all students can, and should, learn, then free market expectations for "winners" and "losers" are denied. Equality renders marketplace competition that destroys competitors unnecessary. Nevertheless, proponents of privatization education sustain policies and practices that exclude and discriminate. A standard-bearer for inequality, free market theory jettisons the burden of equality in favor of an educational playing field that tilts away from the burdens of traditional public schooling.

The Incomplete Obligation

Funding for traditional public education, a sizeable investment from any vantage point, is, nonetheless, an incomplete obligation. Defining adequacy as high minimum quality, manipulating state funding formulas, and ignoring court findings—all represent factors that guarantee incomplete funding for traditional public education.

For instance, "most states provide sufficient resources to their lowest-poverty districts and achieve above-average outcomes. The opposite is true, however, of the highest-poverty districts: they are underfunded vis-à-vis predicted requirements, and their students perform accordingly" (Baker, DiCarlo, and Weber, 2019, 15).

As this discussion suggests, the history of US education is a narrative of incomplete and insufficient pursuit of equity and equality. Investment in traditional public education, therefore, is subject to this narrative and whether the narrative is burden-averse or obligation-engaged.

The influence of democracy, never far removed from any portion of this discussion, is especially relevant in terms of investment, equity, equality, obligation, and burden. "How governments determine what laws and regulations need to be in place depends, largely, on citizens actions in areas of their lives that sometimes involve choices about whether to assume personal costs for a collective good" (Bolsen, 2013, 1).

Emphasizing self-aggrandizement over personal costs for a collective good, free market education proponents battle the burdens which require invest in "the good."

HOW STATES DEAL WITH THE COST OF INVESTMENT

Investment in traditional public education is one of any state's two primary funding obligations. Because a state's contribution to the federal government for Medicare/Medicaid is the other obligation and beyond the control of the state legislature, funding for traditional public education is vulnerable to the free market imperative to reduce taxation devoted to school funding (Swensson, Lehman, and Ellis, 2021).

Before the advent of free market education, state legislatures often subjected school districts to funding formulas that looked like action in Las Vegas. "Stacking the deck to manipulate funding—educational gerrymandering—is a game of chance in which the legislature, like the 'house' in any casino, holds the winning hand" (Swensson, Lehman, and Ellis, 2021, 46–47).

Sometimes, state legislatures slid an ace up their sleeve in the form of mechanisms and machinations as a safeguard to ensure the reduction of the costs of public education.

Mechanisms and Machinations Curtail Investment

A cornucopia of mechanisms and machinations represent the actions taken by many state legislatures to align with free market intentions:

- *Charter Schools*: Charter schools are provided with the same annual per-pupil funding from the state that traditional public schools receive. But, charter schools generally do not have the same expenditures (e.g., transportation, special education services, student/pupil ratio, overhead) that traditional public schools must accommodate. Less service to students is proclaimed as lower cost while it offers marketeers the potential for profit (Swensson, Lehman, and Ellis, 2021).
- *Vouchers*: Voucher funding reduces the total investment a state makes in traditional public education (Bruecker, 2017). The burden of government and the burden of cost represented by traditional US public education are reduced when voucher payments made to private and religious schools are lower than per pupil costs in traditional public schools. Voucher payments often are made to families who can afford and who already pay for private or religious education (Moon and Stewart, 2016).

- *Tax Credits*: "Fiscal subterfuge (e.g., tax credit 'scholarships') gives leeway to private schools and legislatures to claim no state or federal monies fund privatization" (Swensson, Lehman, and Ellis, 2021, 114). Fulfilling low cost as a tenet of free market theory through this ill-disguised fiscal chicanery has the added free market advantage of siphoning off tax dollars that otherwise would be invested in traditional public education.
- *Virtual Education*: Online schools are heralded for the numerous ways they fend off the burden of cost such as "having 2.7 times as many students per teacher (44) compared to the national average" (Molnar et al., 2019, 9). Virtual schools avoid costs associated with brick-and-mortar schools (e.g., utility costs, insurance costs, maintenance costs) but often receive per-pupil payments commensurate with the per-pupil payments to traditional public schools. Profit—never a burden for free market education proponents—is a well-documented feature of online education.
- *For-Profit Schooling*: "Within a decade of the first charter school legislation being passed, for-profit education management organizations (EMOs) became the largest players in the charter school sector" (Baker and Miron, 2015, 7). Privatization schools have been known to offer curtailed services to students (Goldstein, 2017; Shaffer and Dincher, 2020), engage in fraud (Swensson, Lehman, and Ellis, 2021), and close their doors with little or no regard for students and parents but firm allegiance to the principles of marketplace education.
- *State Government Machinations*: Educational gerrymandering occurs when state legislatures fund different school districts in different locations differently (Black, 2019). This selective distribution limits educational cost; direct legislative action also manipulates the dollars available for public schools. "Between 2009–2010 and 2016–2017, a total of forty-two states 'decreased their average annual salary for public school teachers' (Rentner, 2019, p. 4)" (Swensson, Lehman, and Ellis, 2021, 117).
- *Governance & Finance Hocus-Pocus*: Some legislatures facilitate profit and curtail local governance at the same time. These states allow the governing body of a not-for-profit school to "establish a contract with the private management company to both directly manage the school and to engage in all subsidiary contractual agreements; in this arrangement, the employer is the management company, not the school governing board" (Baker and Miron, 2015, 12).

Ohio provides an example of school funding hocus-pocus. "The state does not base the funding formula on any real or objective estimates; it simply fills in the blanks in the formula with numbers that, when multiplied, will equal the preordained amount of money the state is willing to spend" (Black, 2019, 1410).

COVENANT: A BURDEN ON SINGULARITY

Covenant is the relationship between public educators and student-centric intentions that nurtures citizenship in US democracy.

Democracy is a covenant among citizens to balance individual freedom with safety and well-being for all. This relationship is an exchange from which the common good emerges. The values of moral obligation in US public education and the original power of education are among the choices that build covenant.

One representation of "the good" created in such an exchange is *the social contract*. A simple illustration of this unwritten covenant is limited arm-swinging by individuals while walking along the sidewalk in exchange for an unlimited benefit, no broken noses (Swensson and Shaffer, 2020).

On a broader scale, traditional public education that engages all students in the intersection of *how to think* and the moral obligation of public education is "payment required for the public good in U.S. democracy: constraint of a person's right to swing his/her individual needs into the nose of covenant" (Swensson, Ellis, and Shaffer, 2019a, 82).

The social value of this intersection, the original power of education, is expressed when the obligations of traditional public education ensure that "a good public school prepares students for 'the "unfixed" social world for which young people will be learning' (McWilliam, 2008, p. 264)" (Swensson and Shaffer, 2020, 11).

This understanding of the public good invokes the balance required in democracy between covenantal attachment and individual freedom. As Brooks (2017) observes, "freedom without covenant becomes selfishness" and "freedom without connection becomes alienation."

Tossing Covenant Aside

Eliminating burdens like covenant and balance is accomplished when singularity is the ultimate freedom. Covenant stands in the way of singularity because it entails learning for all students which entails the costly burden of sufficient funding for all public schools.

Adherence to singularity eliminates the burden to serve all students and discards the burden of investment in public education. Treating covenant as a burden enables and promotes the falsehood that non-privileged student cohorts are neither worthy nor capable of learning (Worrell, 2014).

THE MORAL OBLIGATION OF PUBLIC EDUCATION

The moral obligation of public education is expressed in the "overarching principles [that] have been agreed on in our society and within the teaching profession—principles dealing with honesty, fairness, protection of the weak, and respect for all people (Clark, 1990, p. 252)" (Campbell, 2008, 602).

These principles speak to the obligations that bind

"education as an ethical profession and a 'thoroughly moral business' (Sockett, 1996, p. 124), [that] is unique by virtue of the exceptional vulnerability and dependence of the primary 'clients'—other people's children—in addition to their non-voluntary presence in [traditional public] schools (Bul, 1993; Colnerud, 2001, 2006; Dickinson, 2001; Soder, 1990)." (Campbell, 2008, 605)

A Thoroughly Moral Business

Public education's moral obligation is grounded in the reciprocal relationship between (1) access to critical habits of mind—identified by Goodlad (1990) as facilitating critical enculturation, providing access to knowledge, inquiry, competence, freedom, and social justice—and (2) the moral purpose of teachers found in ethics and competency so that "what makes teachers' practices morally and ethically meaningful rests on whether core virtues and principles are evidently bound up in their intentions and actions" (Campbell, 2008, 606).

Moral obligation and moral purpose are exercised through connections "between reasoning and social conventions and moral concepts about fairness and human welfare" (Nucci, 2008, 292). Moral obligation and moral purpose, within countless day-to-day interactions and communications, shape student engagement in learning.

The End in Mind for Moral Obligation: "The Good"

"The good" is the end in mind, the function or purpose, of moral obligation. Stated succinctly, "'[u]nless we know the end, the good, we shall have no criterion for rationally deciding what the possibilities are which should be promoted' (Dewey, 1985, p. 94)" (Webster, 2015, 12).

"The good" is an obligation to non-rivalrous and non-excludable intentions for public education (Lee, 2018). Praiseworthy conceptions of "the good" are found in values of moral obligation such as "honesty, a sense of fairness, integrity, compassion, patience, respect, impartiality, care, dedication, and other such core virtues" (Campbell, 2008, 603).

The moral purpose of public educators is found in the actions that express these values.

"The Good," Education, and Democracy

"The good" incorporates, further, the obligation of US public education to democracy. This is an obligation to build the understanding that US citizens are "connected by common concerns about their shared fate, care for the interests of others, and the desire to seek shared principles that enable them to work out differences" (Stitzlein, 2015, 566).

The relationship between US democracy and traditional public education is a historic obligation. Dewey (1916) highlighted this obligation when he wrote that "the devotion of democracy to education is a familiar fact" (41). US public schools are "a central institution of democracy—something that sustains democracy but also, in its best forms, is democracy in action" (Stitzlein, 2015, 564).

The mutual expression of this obligation is found in the instrumental agency of educators, elected officials, and citizens who go about "building a sense of the 'we,' trusting others in shared forms of leadership and knowledge-building, empowering others as publics build capacity to make change, and transcending individualistic frames of knowledge and action (Knight Abowitz, 2014)" (Knight Abowitz, 2018, 11).

Public education is uniquely situated to build a *sense of the "we"* from socially valuable characteristics such as virtue and the values of moral obligation.

On the other hand, privatization education is given carte blanche to separate and exclude. "They narrow who counts as 'we' and restrict how individuals learn to interact across difference, thereby precluding a fully rich and diverse democracy" (Stitzlein, 2015, 571).

A Moral Obligation to Democracy

Moral obligation seeks *intradependence* and mutuality through which a stable democracy is achieved.

How to think and the values of moral obligation of public education engage all students with "the good" as citizenship which is virtue central to America's democracy. As scholars note, "'living together justly' places a clear emphasis on the moral dimensions of citizenship" (Knight Abowitz, 2008, 376).

Webster (2017) recapitulates the function of "the good" as the end in mind for obligations of contemporary public educators. "An end operates like a target or a goal to be aimed at but simultaneously and importantly it also provides direction for the sort of means that are appropriate for *hitting* the target (Dewey, 1985, p. 112)" (Webster, 2015, 8).

TRADITIONAL PUBLIC EDUCATION AS MORAL AGENCY

Conduct associated with and derived from the values of moral obligation is an educator's *moral agency* (Campbell, 2008). These behaviors represent the individual and collective obligation of traditional public educators to express ethical knowledge as a nonnegotiable "moral domain, with its universal set of values and a 'basic core of morality'" (Campbell, 2008, 602).

Dewey (1933) pinpointed the reason that this domain is a nonnegotiable for US public education: It evinces "'the method of democracy, of a positive toleration which mounts to sympathetic regard for the intelligence and personality of others, even if they hold views opposed to ours' (p. 329)" (Kurth-Schai, 2014, 429).

Public educators accept this responsibility as accountability for their obligation, as Campbell (2008) indicates, to have awareness of their own "moral agent state of being" (603). This awareness is a moral/ethical knowledge of virtue and values of moral purpose which underlie the moral agency of day-to-day behaviors in public schools.

Self-Mastery and Character

"The character of the individual teacher is central to the moral nature of education (Luckowski, 1997; Sockett, 1996; Wynne & Ryan, 1997)" (Campbell, 2008, 603). Awareness of character, the awareness of moral agency, is derived from *self-mastery.*

Self-mastery "is the conscious intentional process of gradually taking ownership ('colonizing') of various aspects of the self, including one's emotions, impulses, and dispositions" (Lapsley, 2008, 36). Self-mastery is a progression through which public educators are obliged to take ownership of moral purpose. Educators are obligated to exercise self-mastery because they are responsible for the lives, learning, and futures of all students, which means the reflection and action of educators must express moral agency.

Moral agency "is expressed and revealed in the daily practice of teachers who model, self-regulate, instruct, relate, admonish, and engage" (Campbell, 2008, 608).

Moral agency has no relationship with nor connection to partisan causes and ideological premises (Campbell, 2008). Accepted by public educators, this professional commitment is the obligation to teach *how to think* on behalf of the common good.

INTERPRETING THE OBLIGATIONS
OF PUBLIC EDUCATION

Interpretation can reconfigure the obligations of US public education. Several entities' and actors' interpretations skew how obligation is enacted across the breadth of US public schools:

- *State legislatures* rush through a door opened by state constitutions to create a hodgepodge of interpretations about public education (Imoukhuede, 2019). Interpretation encourages legal and moral commitments to drift, often to the point that ideology substitutes for moral obligation. Interpreting ideology as a doppelganger of moral obligation is synergy of struggle at work.
- *State courts and state legislatures* render conflicting interpretations of the obligations of public education.

The power of legislative interpretations, here declaimed in findings of the Ohio State Supreme Court, can ensure "'that [low-wealth] school districts were starved for funds, lacked teachers, buildings, and equipment, and had inferior educational programs, and that their pupils were being deprived of educational opportunity' (*DeRolph v. State,* 1997, p. 205)" (Sciarra and Hunter, 2017, 7).

Court interpretations like these that call legislatures to task for neglecting a constitutional duty for public education are met with legislative interpretations in response. Legislatures often play cat-and-mouse with these court findings, sometimes for years, without acting in accordance with the court's directives to undo the damage done to students by interpretation (Imoukhuede, 2019).

- *External accountability* contributes interpretive voices about obligation from foundations, think tanks, and other well-funded private entities. These entities—which have no legal authority over traditional public education—engage in conflict with the obligations of traditional public education.

Prominent among these entities is ALEC (American Legislative Exchange Council). "ALEC is part of a larger network of organizations, foundations, and individuals dedicated to creating a free market for U.S. education (Hefling, 2017; Mayer, 2017)" (Swensson, Ellis, and Shaffer, 2019b, 46).

ALEC is "best described as a 'corporate bill mill' that helps conservative state legislators become a vessel for advancing special interest legislation" (Fischer, 2013, 26). The substitution preferences about education alive and well in state legislatures are aided and abetted by the model bills ground out by this mill.

Interpretation in Action: Intentional Impermanence

When a state constitution indicates that the legislature is obliged to provide for public education, the permanence of this obligation seems beyond question. Interpretation, however, has a surprising effect: *intentional impermanence* (Swensson, Lehman, and Ellis, 2021).

Impermanence is grounded in the free market premise that competition between schools leads to the closure of inefficient institutions (Swensson, Ellis, and Shaffer, 2019a). Marketplace education is a realm where schools can "lose" at any time and close permanently.

This is intentional impermanence that leaves students and families in educational limbo and abrogates the constitutional obligation to provide education. Although disconnected from sufficient support for its obligations and faced with sustained marketplace antipathy, traditional public schools are expected to pick up the pieces and enroll the students who bear the burden when a privatization school loses.

Placing the burden of a closed school squarely on the shoulders of students, families, and communities is a consequence of the impermanence-guarantee in free market theory.

Intentional impermanence inverts constitutional obligation in other ways. Popular in many states, for instance, is *the handoff*. "A number of local and state governments in the US have transferred activities and functions from public spheres to private organizations" (Lee, 2018, 4). Handing-off the obligation to educate is a cost-cutting maneuver that also reduces the presence of government.

Private organizations that receive the handoff get state dollars but are under no obligation to verify how the funds are used. The hand-off does not require accountability about the things (e.g., curriculum, instructional methods) natural to education. Free market education is the intentional impermanence of obligation to "the good."

REPRISE: EDUCATIONAL ANTIPATHY

Educational antipathy is the stark Darwinian ethos espoused by proponents of free market education who stipulate that "if you fail to achieve that good life it is your fault" (Brown, 2002, 100). Educational antipathy facilitates the abandonment of obligations for moral agency such as:

- *All students have the capacity to learn:* Educational antipathy assigns *consumer failure* to students of color, students in poverty, students whose first language is not English, and students with special needs (Swensson, Ellis, and Shaffer, 2019a). Aided and abetted by state discrimination (Swensson, Ellis, and Shaffer, 2019a) and racism (Swensson, Lehman, and Ellis, 2021), "less," "deficiency," and "genetic incapacity" are imposed nefariously and intentionally on US students. The educational marketplace employs educational antipathy as if it's common sense.
- *All public schools deserve fiscal sufficiency:* Insufficient funding is educational antipathy built into state funding formulas throughout the nation (Swensson, Lehman, and Ellis, 2021). Underfunding public education, empowering high-wealth districts to raise local taxes, abandoning low-wealth districts whose recourse to local tax increases is limited, and piling on mandates that enforce the limitations of oxymoronic minimal educational adequacy—all are deliberate legislative ploys allied with educational antipathy. Educational antipathy depletes resources and denies access in the name of reducing the perceived burdens of public education.
- *All learning should be equitable:* Students—based on location, ethnicity, race, poverty—are subjected to academic depredations that spring from competition, gerrymandering, and underfunding (Black, 2019; Swensson, Lehman, and Ellis, 2021). Racist assumptions and behaviors blame and exclude students for their lived experience. "Devoted to the success of the market itself and its adherents, privatization proffers *consumer failure* to cohorts of our society that do not fit the vendor-centric, profit-producing, ideology-enhancing agenda written into implementation of the free market" (emphasis original) (Swensson, Ellis, and Shaffer, 2019a, 13).

Purported consumer failure in the educational marketplace is nothing less than the effect of educational antipathy. By marginalizing students, the irresponsibilities of the marketplace give license to bigotry and denial of "the good."

OBLIGATION VS. BURDEN: GOLD OR PYRITE?

Obligations and burdens are as different as pyrite and gold. An ordinary mineral and a precious metal provide educators with a cautionary tale about burden and obligation: the glitter associated with each depends on perspective.

The adage "all that glitters is not gold" speaks to the first-glance similarities between gold and pyrite. Unable to decipher the difference between metal and mineral, many would-be prospectors celebrated striking it rich based merely on glitter. Glittery pyrite, a worthless mineral, is called fool's gold for a reason.

The adherents of both major perspectives go prospecting for what's socially valuable and natural to education. And, just as prospectors must differentiate between pyrite and gold, public educators are obliged to choose between the two major perspectives in terms of the value of the glitter in one or the other.

Differentiating Between Obligation and Burden

To choose privatization education, educators and others react to the glitter in "a set of assumptions built on the economic definition of a public good that views education as only an individual experience sought to fulfill one's unique desires" (Knight Abowitz and Stitzlein, 2018, 34). This is a choice to react to student-centric intentions as a burden. The ideological cookie cutter that is free market theory configures, commodifies, monetizes, and commercializes education and its purpose. Amorality of free market theory is chosen to express the public good as one's unique desires.

To choose traditional public education, educators and others react to the glitter of investment as a commitment to moral purpose and dynamic instruction so that all students acquire successful intelligence, the capacity to meet "the demands of living in a free civil society, . . . [and] develop empathy for others and a commitment to personal responsibility for one's individual actions" (Campbell, 2008, 608). This choice is the obligation to engage all students with *how to think* and the common good.

Determining whether the history of the future of US public education is gold or pyrite, depends, in part, on whether the provision of education for the greater good by society is an obligation or a burden.

Choice about the future of US public education may yield a preselected aggregation of educational pyrite dug from the tenets of free market theory. Or, choice about the future of US public education may be an engagement with the gold standard of educational function in pursuit of learning and the common good for all students.

Educators may choose stasis and singularity, relying on intentions as the only arbiter of choice. Or, educators can perceive choice as a whole that is more than the sum of its parts.

One way or the other, choice will write the narrative for the history of the future of US public education. Hanging in the balance of choice is the original power of education to foster "cognitive behaviors necessary and sufficient to honesty, social justice, public liberty, truth, and the excellence of integrity (Strike, 2008)" (Swensson and Shaffer, 2020, 24).

As discussion about the arbiters of choice suggests, struggle over the purpose of America's public education is built in to the pathways to the future that lie before public educators. But, the intensity of this struggle and the consequences of educational choice only begin with intentions.

Public educators, and any individual concerned about America's struggle over choice about learning, must delve into choice well beyond intentions and the implications derived from discussing the arbiters of choice. The full measure of choice about the history of the future of traditional US public education is explored in the next two chapters in terms of *the submerged state, attenuation, public dissonance,* and *the public.*

Chapter 7

Public Education

Submerged and Attenuated

EMAIL
To: Traditional Public Educators
Fr: Several Retired Colleagues
Re: Roadblocks

To choose the road taken to the future, educators, parents/caregivers, and others deserve an opportunity to reflect on factors beyond the arbiters of choice that influence history and, thus, the purpose, policies, and practices of US public education.

Composing the history of the future of traditional public educators from intentions alone isn't enough. The narrative cannot be complete without attention paid to the roadblocks erected to thwart public education as a journey.

Two roadblocks—*the submerged state* and *attenuation*—are not the only obstacles in the path of traditional public education. However, these barriers represent factors that public educators cannot afford to ignore if a student-centric narrative is to be chosen.

The submerged state lurks below the surface of democracy in "policies that channel public money through private delivery mechanisms" (Hackett, 2017, 464). Attenuation is the intentional distancing of the state from entities including US public education.

The submerged state and attenuation tie educators and instruction to state standards for annual testing and minimum quality as adequacy. As shared in the upcoming chapter, these are the means for distancing students from learning in public schools.

Moreover, intentionally placing students at a remove from learning is tantamount to creating distance, instead of connection, as a goal of education. Choosing free market education is a choice to promote distance between government and public education, between education and learning, and between learning and citizenship in US democracy.

Fundamentally, the choice public educators have about the future of our profession and its impact on students and society ought to involve much more than just analysis of intentions in one major perspective or the other.

Public educators, all of us, are faced with a far more meaningful choice about a future narrative than at first it may appear.

The meaning of this choice lies in the difference between connection and disconnection. Or, put in context of US democracy and citizenship, we are choosing between *the public* and *public dissonance* for the narrative about the history of the future of US education.

SHOULD PUBLIC EDUCATION CONNECT OR DISCONNECT?

From mandatory courses about America's history and government to celebrations laden with patriotic themes, traditional public schools in the twenty-first century connect students with the nation's heritage. From learning to read and reading to learn, to Advanced Placement (AP) and International Baccalaureate (IB) courses, traditional public schools connect students with learning.

Connections, however, are not the sole narrative written in the twenty-first century for the history of the future of public education. Two relatively unheralded forces are in play that compose a narrative of disconnection.

Manifestations of Disconnection

Despite the efforts of traditional public educators to ensure that student-centric intentions begin the connections facilitated by formal learning experiences, *the submerged state* and *attenuation* work persistently to foster disconnection.

Hackett (2017) identifies the *submerged state* as "indirect government subsidies and benefits such as tax expenditures: policies that channel public money through private delivery mechanisms and through tax subsidies, rebates, and credits rather than direct governmental spending (Grever, Flinders, and Van Thiel, 1999; Mettler, 2009; Surrey, 1970)" (464).

The submerged state is employed to disconnect government from its constitutional role in support of public education. State legislatures give themselves license to look the other way to divert funding from public education to privatization education.

Taking funding away from public schools eliminates connections between students and learning, higher-order thinking, and citizenship. The submerged state torpedoes the Good Ship US Public Education and sinks the connections intended for a life-enhancing journey.

Under these circumstances, US education becomes nothing less than the choice to disregard those meant to book passage on this vessel: students. The submerged state finances a "destination" for education natural to the intentions of free market schooling (Swensson, Lehman, and Ellis, 2021).

Funding a Destination

Free market education is a destination anchored by "scholarship funds." Often referred to as tax credit scholarships, these manifestations of the submerged state are created as private entities to receive "donations" from businesses or individuals in lieu of the taxes that these "scholarship donors" would otherwise pay to support traditional public education.

Quietly eroding state taxation to support traditional public schools, the submerged state permits donations to constitute a tax credit. In this way, the submerged state permits the payment of tuition directly or indirectly for students at private and religious schools.

Submerged programs (e.g., tax credits, "scholarship organizations") stealthily distance free market education from *the public* to dodge potential legal challenges when religiously affiliated schools benefit from this funding (Hackett, 2017).

Funding manipulations channeled through the submerged state allow ideologues and politicians "to emphasize the indirectness of the aid programs so as to maintain an official separation between Church and State" (Hackett, 2017, 466).

Tax credits, using Florida as an example, can be *deeply submerged* when "corporations are entitled to redirect up to 100 percent of their corporate income or insurance premium tax liability annually to a 'Scholarship Funding Organization'" (Hackett, 2017, 470).

Private action, in this case, submerges the connection between public education and state government. This becomes a paradoxical transformation when consumer relations proclaim this manipulation as permission "to undertake actions deemed to have an important public purpose" (Hackett, 2017, 466). Separation extolled as if it's an important public connection is nothing less than the emphasis of free market theory on preferred customers and singularity. Privatization education advances the paradox that inequity serves everyone.

Lurking below the surface, away from the view of most citizens, the submerged state advantages the intentions of free market schooling. Educators and citizens cannot see the periscope of free market theory because it's shrouded in the dense fog of impenetrable language of statutes that conceal the submerged state (Swensson and Shaffer, 2020).

Attacking on behalf of privatization education, submerged state policies torpedo funding, intentions, and purpose for traditional public schools (Sciarra and Hunter, 2015).

ATTENUATION: DISTANCING PUBLIC EDUCATION FROM ITSELF

The submerged state separates traditional public education from government. The process responsible for policy that increases the distance between government and an entity like public education is referred to as *attenuation* (Hackett, 2017).

In practical terms, attenuation is the deliberate effort to distance traditional public education from itself.

When policies eliminate local school boards or otherwise distance school governance and/or school funding from *the public, attenuation is underway.* Distancing traditional public education from government opens ideological space for adult-centric intentions (e.g., mechanisms, low-cost, singularity, profit, absentee governance). Attenuation is invoked when charter school governance is placed in the hands of board members who have no other connection with or involvement in the community served by the school (Giroux, 2014).

Distance and disconnection grow when "processes of privatization in education and commodification of schooling fundamentally challenge the two conditions of non-excludability and non-rivalrousness essential to define a public good (Labaree, 1997; Lubienski, 2006)" (Lee, 2018, 14). Attenuation is the intentional distancing of the public good from US students.

Attenuation: In Defense of Free Market Schooling

Attenuation manufactures schooling that is rivalrous and exclusive. Attenuation establishes buffer zones against connection. If circumstances in society, or actions by government, *increase* connection between government and America's schooling, attenuation is an effective, free market-enhancing, defense.

During the latter half of the twentieth century and into the early decades of the twenty-first century, for instance, federal legislation and court decisions increased connection between government and public education.

Federal legislation and court decisions increased diversity, equity, access, and adequacy in US public life and traditional public education (Carey and

Harris, 2016; Goldstein, 2015; Levin, 2002). As a result, distance between government and US public education shrank.

In response to these threats, free market adherents and others rallied with attenuation. State-level legislation, guided by model bills infused with free market intentions, responded to increase the distance between public education and federal government-initiated connections (Levin, 2002).

Segregation academies, free market mechanisms, submerged state funding schemes, and standardized testing were among the weapons of attenuation deployed in defense of privatization education, discrimination, and a restricted role for education in the public sector (Suitts, 2019).

Attenuation multiplies the damage done to students who face life-costs. Distancing learners from capacities that facilitate connection, attenuation undercuts meaning-making that, otherwise, grows in the intersection of *how to think* and the common good.

FOREGROUNDING THE MEANS OF ATTENUATION

Standardized tests measure connections between schooling and adult-centric intentions and, thus, serve to enforce and defend attenuation between students and learning. This is a state of affairs where, as Webster (2017) observes, "there is a foregrounding of the *means* of measuring and a relegation into the background of the *ends* or purposes of education" (emphasis original) (334).

Standardized testing is the machinery for foregrounding means (the disconnections of free market theory) and backgrounding student-centric connections. In the foreground of US education, extruded from this machine, are test scores that validate the extent to which productivity is in the foreground of a school.

Productivity in the guise of test scores generates either praise or condemnation of schools and school districts in terms exclusive to the principles of free market theory. These expectations and the sanctions that accompany them exist to distance public education from *the public*. Combined with the submerged state, this emphasis on means instead of ends or purpose in public education maximizes disconnection and distance.

Nurturing Attenuation

Legislators nurture attenuation (often in model bills drafted by ALEC to enact the submerged state) via statutes that confirm and strengthen "the vast—and growing—governmental role in subsidizing private-sector social benefits" (Hackett, 2017, 465).

The carapace of reform protects the distancing of tax dollars away from "government schools" (aka traditional public education) to marketplace schools. Attenuation facilitates, and the submerged state hides, provision of state funding to private religious schools.

Educational gerrymandering further facilitates attenuation. When school districts are placed at a distance from sufficient funding for teaching and learning, high-wealth school districts compensate with local funding to close this gap. But, other school districts, unable to fill the funding gap created by a state-created shortfall, have no choice but to distance students from learning by eliminating courses and services.

Less visible than educational gerrymandering is attenuation created when states' budgets prioritize business over traditional public education. Indiana's state and local governments between 2010 and 2020, for instance, "spent $5 billion on tax incentives for businesses—while adding a meager $17 million to the budgets of colleges and universities" (Briggs, 2022, 24A). The result, observers note, is underperforming public education and a dearth of well-educated employees (Briggs, 2022).

Attenuation, thus, reinforces the oxymoron of high minimum quality that serves as the working definition for adequacy in US public education. Stretching the distance between state government and its obligations for public education, the effect of attenuation is to multiply the inadequacies and insufficiencies that submerge learning and deny the common good.

Attenuation of *the Public*

Citizenship and the common good come to a standstill when attenuation increases the distance between US education and student-centric intentions that pursue "the good."

Attenuation is a storm widening the distance between government and citizenship and between traditional public education and its historic purpose.

As scholars observe, the storm of attenuation aggravates disconnection within America's public that is "now largely diffused, inchoate, unable to conceive and articulate forcefully, an alternative, more genuinely democratic vision of educational reform" (Granger, 2008, 222). When separation increases in society and education, the common good is blown off course.

A diffused, inchoate, public is vulnerable to the entreaties of consumer relations and the submerged state masquerading as reform. The allure assigned to increasing distance between individuals and government is enhanced when the submerged state and attenuation combine within:

- State Standards for Testing

Frequently, politicians, educators, and scholars contend that an adequate public school is meant to "offer students a genuine opportunity to meet state academic learning standards" (Sciarra and Hunter, 2015, 3). Although standards are often identified as solid gold learning, compared with learning *how to think*, state standards are nothing more than deposits of educational pyrite.

Educationally inert, standards may be aspirational but, as the New Jersey Supreme Court observed, "'the standards themselves do not ensure any substantive level of achievement' (*Abbott IV*, 1994, p. 417)" (Sciarra and Hunter, 2015, 14). Standards and the tests that incorporate them hide the distance between students and learning.

- Minimum Adequacy

  Observers, scholars, and educators bemoan the inadequacy of funding for public education and the inadequate student achievement associated with public schools (Sciarra and Hunter, 2015). But, as this discussion indicates, adequacy is a term whose glitter is only the "minimum." High minimum quality, a collection of disconnections pretending to be adequacy, increases the distance between public education and learning, equity, sufficiency, and the common good.

THE DAMAGE DONE BY DISTANCE: ILLUSIONS, DISCONNECTIONS, AND CONTRADICTIONS

America's contradictions, as this discussion illustrates, are symbolized by the nation's divergent views throughout history about the role of the public sector. Contradictions in US education mirror the nation's divisions and are reflected in the struggle over choice about learning.

The purpose of traditional US public education, at its best, is to engage all students with the capacities to make sense of contradictions and conflict in society to the end that the common good is realized. But, when the promise of learning for the common good is contradicted by attenuation and disconnection, US education becomes an illusion.

Choose or Avoid Illusion?

Attenuation and disconnection erode the purpose of traditional US public education. With distance imposed between learners and student-centric intentions, education becomes an illusion.

The late congressman John Lewis (2012) described how the contradictions that riddle the history of the nation and its public education detain students of color and students in poverty within education as an illusion. Lewis explained how education and its promises of a better future undercut the capabilities of students.

Disconnected from funding, challenging learning materials, safe modern school buildings, and access to courses necessary for college admissions, students in public schools where insufficiences abound embrace personal goals and aspirations that are snuffed out when the promises of public education become little more than a mirage. Distancing education from the lives of cohorts of US students has already exacted a societal price that advocates of traditional US public education, like Congressman Lewis, seek to end.

The ethos of separation (e.g., singularity, segregation) and subterfuge (e.g., the submerged state, hidden enrollment requirements) fostered in free market theory as acceptable ways of "doing business" represent factors that impose illusion on the purpose and practices of public education. Business, in this case, is tantamount to deliberately distancing the narrative for the history of the future of public education from equity.

When equity is an illusion, when sufficient funding is an illusion, when learning is an illusion, when adequacy is an illusion, and when connections between democracy and US schools are an illusion, learning for all students and meaningful citizenship in US democracy are purposes and outcomes attenuated from the foreground of the lives of too many of America's students.

THE FUTURE OF US PUBLIC EDUCATION

The future narrative about US public education is being written by the choices public educators make in the twenty-first century. This narrative of education's history will be reflected and adapted to meet the future needs and interests of those responsible for public education (Otremba, 2020).

The history of the future of traditional public education, thus, is the narrative of choices made by contemporary public educators and the authorities who oversee teaching and learning. Present-day choices will be the guidance, the content, that shapes the future narrative of public education.

If Adult-Centric Intentions Are Written

Submerged and attenuated, privatization education is a premium item in a marketplace where stasis is for sale. Illusions are foisted upon students and *the public* when adherents of free market theory generate insufficient funding for learning throughout US schools. The marketplace prioritizes separation to sustain existing contradictions in education while prompting reflection and action that expand educational denial when attenuation is a priority.

Instead of serving *the public*, the marketplace is home to the public dissonance inherent in illusions and the denial of equity. Illusion reigns when denial and distance enforce adult-centric intentions.

If Student-Centric Intentions Are Written

The relationship between public education and US democracy is a time-honored reciprocity (Dewey, 1916).

Public schools, when all is said and done, are "places of interactive learning and building social relationships. To be successful, they must accommodate individual interests and differences in a way that also meets society's common needs and promotes certain shared values and principles" (Knight Abowitz and Stitzlein, 2018, 34).

Public educators accept these obligations to connect and build student-centric intentions in the twenty-first century and influence the future narrative for US public education. Articulating and serving the relationship between the principles of democracy and the promises of public education means ending the distances and illusions perpetrated in the name of free market theory.

What About the Roadblocks?

The roadblocks in the path of a student-centric narrative for US education— e.g., the submerged state, attenuation—appear formidable. Constructed with ideological and political tools, these barriers obstruct the connections for which traditional public education is responsible.

Distance and separation limit student engagement with *how to think* and the values of the moral obligation of traditional public education. Separating public education from purpose, funding, and *the public* perpetrates anew the illusion of learning that so many proponents of traditional public education have labored to erase.

With this in mind, traditional public educators may despair over the future and what it might take to connect all students with the original power of education in a narrative for the history of the future of public schooling. Giving in to the perception that traditional public education is battling overwhelming odds is not, however, the only option available.

Although discussion in the next chapter about public dissonance may increase the concerns that traditional public educators have about the future, the chapter also sheds light on *the public* and reasserts the impact and agency that public educators, all of us, have as we attend to the future that all students deserve.

Chapter 8

Public Dissonance or
Public Things?

EMAIL
To: Traditional Public Educators
Fr: Your Performing Arts Colleagues
Re: Which "Public" Is Our Middle Name?

Most public educators, along with most parents and caregivers, think that *educational choice* is the selection of privatization education. This view of educational choice, however, is just as flawed as America's definition of adequacy in public education.

The upcoming chapter sheds light on the misrepresentation of *educational choice* that afflicts contemporary public education. Educational choice is ballyhooed by its proponents as a "right" and a "freedom" that traditional public education does not permit.

But, upon closer inspection, educational choice is nothing less than the ascendency of *public dissonance* to disable *public things.*

Public dissonance is disdain for public things expressed in the deliberate denial of the common good (Hostetler, 2003; Swensson, Ellis, and Shaffer, 2019a). Public things "are those material objects and spaces that are a shared and intractable part of democratic life" (Knight Abowitz, 2018, 8).

Importantly, public things do not entail "the seeking of unanimity or harmony, but rather, a meeting of different, independent perspectives emerging 'from the heart of life in all its expansive and messy disarray, not as consensus, but as a comingling of viewpoints'" (Ciulla et al., 2018, 9).

But, disconnections created by public dissonance and sold in the educational marketplace (e.g., attenuation, competition) are meant to disassemble the relationship between *the public* and public things.

Public dissonance is default choice for adherents of free market education. Distancing privatization education from the intentions of traditional public education, public dissonance is the intentional disruption of balance between public things and individual rights.

Which "public" (e.g., public dissonance, public things) is the "middle name" given to America's public education? The answer to this question will be written when public educators enact an understanding of our transformative role in educational choice.

The upcoming chapter examines the implications and consequences of choosing one "middle name" or the other.

THE MISREPRESENTATION OF
EDUCATIONAL CHOICE

A counterfeit version of *educational choice* occupies the attention of twenty-first-century America. Co-opted by proponents of free market theory, educational choice is assumed to define a parent's or caregiver's selection among marketplace options such as mechanisms and privatization schools.

Such a selection is nothing more than unchoice, a singular ideological destination masquerading as a bustling marketplace of choices for schooling. During the past several decades, proponents of traditional public education have ceded this misrepresentation of educational choice to free market proponents.

Will the Real *Educational Choice* Please Stand Up!

To take this discussion beyond misrepresentation requires a brief glimpse of historic television entertainment. Long before the digital age, US television audiences delighted in a program called *To Tell the Truth*.

Three guests appeared on each episode and claimed to be the same individual, someone who had made a little-publicized but worthy or unique accomplishment. Two of the guests were imposters.

A panel of four celebrities questioned the guests. But, the guests' answers were deliberate attempts to fool the panel.

After asking questions, each celebrity announced which guest was "really" the accomplished individual. Once the celebrities shared their guesses, "Will the real (name of individual) please stand up?" rang out, and the truth was revealed when the actual accomplished individual stood.

In the twenty-first century, although this program has staged a TV comeback, there doesn't seem to be much need to guess the true "identity" of educational choice. Conventional wisdom identifies the "truth" about educational choice: parental selection of privatization education.

Standing Up

But, educational choice is much more than mere school selection. Educational choice is a struggle to determine "the line beyond which the state cannot interfere with the precious right of individual liberty of conscience, association, or expression" (Knight Abowitz, 2008, 365).

Like one side in a tug-of-war, privatization education adherents pull this line as far as possible toward the tenets of free market theory to minimize or erase the extent to which public education "interferes" with individual liberty.

Egregious examples of this "interference," according to some critics, is found in units of study that cover the Holocaust, immigration, and American identities that hide "the signs of liberal brainwashing" (Molloy, 2022).

Adherents of traditional public education pull this line in the opposite direction toward balancing the rights of individuals with the common good of society.

For the two major perspectives, educational choice is either (1) the necessity of a "public" to guide or govern balance between rights and responsibilities, or (2) enacting the singular rights embedded in free market theory as a declaration of "individual good" (Knight Abowitz, 2008).

Default Choice: A Second Look

Free market theory dictates that public education, or any governmental entity, interferes with individual liberty. To eliminate interference with individual liberty, free market proponents employ *public dissonance*.

Public dissonance, stipulated for this discussion, is disdain for public things expressed in the deliberate denial of the common good. Non-interference, antipathy, attenuation, subterfuge, and the synergy of struggle are among the marketplace battalions marshalled to disconnect *the public* from education.

PUBLIC DISSONANCE: THE SUM OF INTENTIONS

A throwback to the disconnected role of the public sector enacted under the Articles of Confederation, public dissonance exacerbates the struggle over the purpose of public education in America. Selecting singularity and self-aggrandizement for the role of the public sector opens the door to a narrative in which public dissonance is socially valuable and US education is virtue-free.

Self-aggrandizement and competition justify public dissonance as a means. Sustaining inequity, promoting enrollment discrimination, and validating minimums as adequacy in public education—all, and more, create dissonance that disrupts public things in favor of the educational marketplace (Swensson and Shaffer, 2020).

Concocting Common Sense and FUD

Public dissonance, under the guise of free market schooling, is promoted via several "common sense" assumptions of marketeers:

- *It's Common Sense to Separate from Public Things:* Public dissonance is a consumer relations message that (1) existing public schools are inadequate and (2) reform of this government entity requires separation of individuals from the intrusion of public things. This message offers common sense from a privatization perspective in its indictment: traditional US public education is the soul of inefficient bureaucracy and governmental overreach (Chubb and Moe, 1990).
- *Turn to FUD:* Fear, uncertainty, and doubt (FUD) are the calling cards of public dissonance. FUD ensures that function follows form. "FUD about traditional public education 'makes people so desperate that they will seek out unproven alternatives. It makes the public gullible when they hear phony claims about miracle [choice] schools' (Moyers, 2014)" (Swensson, Ellis, and Shaffer, 2019b, 119). So prevalent, malign, and influential is FUD that adversaries of traditional public education proclaim that public schools practice indoctrination and "groom" students for unethical purposes (Molloy, 2022). Calumny like this is designed as FUD that disconnects parents and caregivers from traditional public education. FUD not only disassembles the purpose of traditional US public education but it also decimates the morale of traditional public educators (Herron, 2022b).
- *Ignore the Low Achievement Behind the Curtain:* Voucher programs in Indiana, Louisiana, and Ohio, for instance, have "negative or neutral effects on student achievement" (Boser, Boser, and Roth, 2018, "An Overview," para. 2).
- *Ignore Costly Students:* The sixty-two voucher programs in twenty-nine states (as of 2019) "provide public funding to schools that can legally remove or refuse to serve certain students altogether" (Fiddiman and Yin, 2019, "The Danger," para. 1). "Charter schools in competitive markets protect their market position by opting for less costly and more easily educated students, and by excluding students from low-income or single-parent families" (Lee, 2018, 13).

Claims about "common sense" and FUD upend connections between citizens, parents, and caregivers with the common good. Public dissonance—distrust, disconnection, distancing—increases when free market intentions are financed by state legislatures.

As this discussion illustrates, public dissonance is delivered in massive quantities through educational gerrymandering (Black, 2019). Traditional public education is attenuated from its purpose in this omnipresent public dissonance and its tendency to:

- arbitrarily drive down the estimated cost of educating students;
- consistently pick low fiscal supplements for at-risk students;
- conveniently exclude inflation increases and other fixed costs over time; and
- intentionally shift excessive and unrealistic funding burdens onto local districts (Black, 2019, 1396).

Public Dissonance: Augmenting Default Choice

Public dissonance disconnects *the public* from US education, denies instrumental agency to public educators, confounds learning on behalf of all US students, and validates the intentions that galvanize the role of the public sector to disconnection and singularity.

Public dissonance is exercised, for instance, when singularity initiatives lead to legislation that censors reading materials and restricts topics for classroom discussion (Powell, 2021; Herron, 2022a).

From a historical vantage point, public dissonance reflects the disdain for the common good fostered in the United States by the forces of nativism, injustice, and exclusion. Free market theory augments these forces through mechanisms, attenuation, and singularity. Public dissonance represents external forces and factors that augment the simple pathway that is default choice.

Public Dissonance and Its Priorities

Disdainful of public things, public dissonance prioritizes the myriad disconnections made socially valuable by singularity. For example, management organizations seeking profit, discriminatory enrollment practices, survival-of-the-fittest competition between schools and among students, state funding for religious school attendance, private entities manufacturing legislation to promote free market education—all are contemporary creatures of public dissonance.

Public dissonance is applied when the threats inherent in student-centric intentions are identified. Traditional US public education, thus, is a "loser" because it is costly and inefficient. Traditional US public education is a threat that erodes individual liberty (e.g., school attendance areas, required vaccinations, court-ordered desegregation).

Public dissonance weaponizes free market theory. Threats to adult-centric intentions are met with imbalance. Individuals (their rights, proclivities, biases, and priorities) outweigh any and all iterations of the common good (Chubb and Moe, 1990).

PUBLIC THINGS AND *THE PUBLIC*: BEYOND THE SUM OF INTENTIONS

Education-as-journey entails support for and engagement with the evolving nature of public things. Public things, as discussed earlier, "are those material objects and spaces that are a shared and intractable part of democratic life" (Knight Abowitz, 2018, 8).

From this understanding emerges *public selection.* Stipulated for this discussion, public selection is instrumental agency necessary and sufficient to choose balance as a public thing.

Public Selection of Public Things

Traditional US public education is a public thing (Swensson and Lehman, 2021), a space dedicated to balance between individual and common "goods."

Balance is an intractable part of democratic life. Balance is not, however, an intention or even a disposition. Rather, balance develops when *the public* acquires the capacity to interrelate *how to think* with the values of the moral obligation of public education and with intelligences (analytic, creative, practical) necessary and sufficient to sustain the fundamental principles of justice and equity in America's democracy.

The purpose of traditional public educators is to teach this capacity to all students. As they do so, public educators accept responsibility for and are *accountable for* a professional balance expressed in understanding that:

- Public things do not entail "the seeking of unanimity or harmony, but rather, a meeting of different, independent perspectives emerging 'from the heart of life in all its expansive and messy disarray, not as consensus, but as a comingling of viewpoints'" (Ciulla et al., 2018, 9). Traditional public education is a choice of the original power of education where all students engage with *how to think* and the moral obligation of education to learn that comingling viewpoints is socially valuable in a democracy.
- As a public thing, US education "must accommodate individual interests and differences in a way that also meets society's common needs and

promotes certain shared values and principles" (Knight Abowitz and Stitzlein, 2018, 35). This view of public education reflects the American Historical Association's statement that "'the ideal of informed citizenship necessitates an educated public'" (Silverstein, 2021).

Public selection entails an obligation to US democracy. "Sustaining democracy is a balancing act of rights and responsibilities, where citizens earn positive and negative liberties by virtue of citizenship but must also fulfill duties to their state that protect those liberties for others" (Stitzlein, 2015, 569).

In the intersection of *how to think* and the values of the moral obligation of public education, individuals acquire virtue (arête) necessary and sufficient for reflection and action that balances rights and responsibilities in democracy. This outcome of traditional public education is *the public.* Fostering this outcome, educators enact public selection.

Choosing Public Selection

Public selection is the commitment of public educators to "foster the child's construction of a worldview based on 'goodwill' (Arsenio and Lover, 1995) characterized by the presumption that social life operates for the most part according to basic moral principles of fairness and mutual respect" (Nucci, 2008, 298–99).

Connecting, bringing *the public* and democracy closer together, public educators are on the cusp of deconstructing the process of attenuation. To curtail stasis and limit the effect of public dissonance, *the public* is an expression of the common good. In part, the common good emerges when *how to think* prioritizes the choice of public things.

The public is nurtured via moral purpose that articulates the balance between principles of America's republic. *The public* expresses the relationship between traditional public education and America's democracy. These relationships are the choice of a connected role for traditional public education in the public sector.

Learning, *the public, democracy, and the common good grow together and, in so doing, offer connected and evolving options for balancing "the good" with individual rights. Exercising balance via public selection, traditional public educators eschew default choice and write a narrative filled with public things for the history of the future of public education.*

REFORM: PUBLIC DISSONANCE
HIDDEN IN PLAIN SIGHT

The public is an inconvenient lesson, an expression of connection anathema to privatization. Public dissonance maximizes individual liberty at the expense of balance in *the public*.

Reform is the cover story behind which the responsibility for public relations conceals the impact of public dissonance. Reform speaks to "fixing" the grievances levied against traditional public education by proponents of free market schooling.

Reform nurtures the belief that what's natural to public education is individual benefit.

Public dissonance is ready-made reform packaged in disconnections manufactured by entities like ALEC (American Legislative Exchange Council). Reform is prepackaged in model bills from ALEC and provided to state legislatures. These cookie cutter statutes provide

> reform and freedom in U.S. schooling [that] comes to the fore via free market agenda items including reducing education cost/taxes, deconstructing teacher unions, establishing profit-making opportunities for free market advocates, and installing mechanisms to enable school choice (Underwood & Mead, 2012). (Swensson, Ellis, and Shaffer, 2019a, 46)

Reform is intentional imbalance throughout US education leveraged so only the "fittest" survive. The "fittest" in free market education are identified in free market theory as individuals (often privileged, wealthy, White) most able to benefit from a winner-take-all schooling.

Reform is a consumer relations label that connotes "something better than" existing public education. But reform is nothing less than public dissonance hiding in plain sight.

This "something better" is free market proponents foisting default choice on the history of the future of public schooling. "Missing in the ideological embrace of choice for choice's sake is any suggestion of the public school as a public good—as a centering locus for a community and as a shared pillar of the commonweal, in which all citizens have an investment" (Mead, 2016).

WHEN PUBLIC THINGS ARE DISTASTEFUL

Proponents of free market education have "a keen distaste for all things public and prefer the speed, efficiency, and individualization of the market for guiding state policies, economic or educational" (Knight Abowitz, 2008, 357).

Public things, from this point of view, are too slow, too inefficient, and too diverse. To rid US education of its status as a public thing, free market proponents disconnect teaching and learning from public things and public life. "More careful shopping by students and parents may be all that is required to spur an educated populace, the public good that is sought through education" (Shaw, 2010, 252).

The call of reform enables privatization proponents to claim that individual "shopping" decisions are the public good. *The public* is recast as individual prerogative.

Shopping-as-education serves as a latter-day iteration of *noblesse oblige.* Free market proponents grant permission to shop to limited participants. The marketplace for education ensures that the dissonance of "privatization" (e.g., rivalrousness, exclusivity) multiplies disconnections between winning and losing individuals and between individuals and their role as *the public.*

Distaste for public things, public selection, and *the public* is evinced in an admixture of free market principles and devices. For example, ideologues "mobilize in support of submerged programs because they favor private parental choice and seek to weaken or attenuate the connection between government and education (Bedrick, Butcher, and Bolick, 2016; Institute for Justice, 2016; Lips and Butcher, 2015)" (Hackett, 2017, 474).

Invisible to many, the submerged state fits snugly into the ideology of free market education. Distaste for public things, a misrepresentation of choice as a linear process, is exclusionary to the point that marketplace education becomes an arena where individuals are attenuated from each other.

Instead of "citizenship viewed as a commitment to a set of principles rather than a shared identity" (Knight Abowitz, 2008, 368), public dissonance attenuates predetermined cohorts of citizens (e.g., enrollees in free market schooling) from commitment to principles of democracy central to the greater good.

The intentions of free market theory offer the shared identity (one benefit of synergy of struggle) that matters most for the proponents of privatization education. With learning relegated to a role subservient to the tenets of free market theory, the primary purpose of marketplace education is ideological.

THE ROAD TO FUNCTIONALLY PUBLIC EDUCATION

As Knight Abowitz (2008) observes, "the public is, in a sense, merely opposite of what is private; not enclosed, not hidden, not exclusive" (359).

To this end, public selection gives public educators the opportunity to take teaching and learning beyond the destination of default choice of adult-centric intentions to education that is *functionally public* (Stitzlein, 2015). "Functionally public schools strive to develop a sense of 'we' collectively, but also an understanding of the well-being of individuals and their ability to pursue their own happiness" (Stitzlein, 2015, 569).

Choosing public things entails pursuit of *the public* in education to build "a sense of the 'we,' trusting others in shared forms of leadership and knowledge-building, empowering others as publics build capacity to make change, and transcending individualistic frames of knowledge and action (Knight Abowitz, 2014)." (Knight Abowitz, 2018, 11).

Public selection arises when the professional capabilities of traditional public educators foster teaching and learning that leads to the balance between personal liberty and citizenship responsibilities which is the common good of both freedom and the cost of freedom.

Public Things for Public Life

Simply put, the distinguishing characteristics of a public thing like traditional US public education are that it must be available to everyone whether they pay taxes or not (non-excludable) and that one individual's use of or involvement with this public good cannot prevent any other person from the same use or involvement (non-rival) (Lee, 2018).

From these distinguishing characteristics emerge the public thing, traditional US public education, that fosters *public life*. Public life in US democracy, again, is not about universal agreement. Nor is it an arid space in which intellectual and creative differences cannot exist.

"Public life will never be able to dispense with antagonism for it concerns public action and the formation of collective identities. It attempts to constitute a 'we' in a context of diversity and conflict (Mouffe, n.d., para. 4)" (Knight Abowitz, 2018, 2). Public life requires citizens whose public education facilitates reflection and action necessary and sufficient for "we" in the context of America's democracy.

The original power of education engages all students to constitute a "we" that is the core of public life. The original power of education endows *the public* with capacities required to accommodate antagonism amid the formation of collective identities in the context of the diversity of US democracy.

The ongoing work of public educators to ensure that *how to think* engages all students with the social value of the principles of democracy and the values of moral obligation writes a narrative for the collective "we" of public life in public things.

In contrast, public dissonance eschews public action and collective identities and prioritizes the inevitable disharmony when competition in a marketplace strives for singularity. Choosing to isolate learning in comfort zones of free market theory and choosing to remove individuals from relationships necessary for the common good, proponents of marketplace education exercise educational choice as disdain and dissonance conveys the "public" of education's middle name.

Chapter 9

What Could Be More Simple
than Educational Choice?

EMAIL
To: Traditional Public Educators
Fr: This Year's Group of Retirees
Re: Student Futures and Gestalt of Choice

Public educators, all of us, face a choice about the narrative for the history of the future of public education, either

1. the destination of free market schooling,

or

2. the journey of traditional public education.

Privatization education proponents revel in free market schooling as the simpler, therefore better, choice. For adherents of privatization education there is no need for an epic struggle about choice for learning in US education when familiar free market patterns lead smoothly to *default choice*. Tipping the scales, public dissonance, attenuation, and the submerged state ensure that adult-centric intentions determine choice about educational choice.

But, teaching and learning are not simple. Public things in a democracy, like US education, are complex, cloaked in uncertainties and unknowns. There is no easy pathway to *how to think* on behalf of the common good. For traditional public educators, however, there is student-centric professionalism accessed via Gestalt of Choice.

Gestalt of Choice is professional engagement with a student-centric future for US public education. To conceptualize Gestalt of Choice, educators can take a cue from the work of renowned twentieth-century graphic artist M. C. Escher.

Escher's work depicting impossibly juxtaposed stairways suggests the complexity of education as a journey. Escher's image provides public educators with a visual metaphor for the professional engagement with instruction facilitated by Gestalt of Choice.

Gestalt of Choice is an educator's reflection and action necessary and sufficient to access and enact instruction that delivers the original power of education, *how to think,* and the common good. Gestalt of Choice takes on added value for student learning when teachers use it to enhance, challenge, and expand meaning-making in response to student learning.

The next chapter explores meaning-making as the goal of instruction generated through Gestalt of Choice.

THE ALLURE OF DEFAULT CHOICE

The intentions and purpose of marketplace schooling evoke the human propensity to identify, classify and seek familiar patterns that lead to default selections and actions (Ritchart and Perkins, 2005).

Free market theory is a mass of familiar patterns (e.g., adult-centric intentions) that simplify selections and actions (e.g., mechanisms, state-sponsored discrimination). Default selections offer familiarity rooted in family, income, and/or race.

Not only does a marketplace for privatization education prioritize the ascendancy of family values as the centerpiece of education (DeBray-Pelot, Lubienski, and Scott, 2007), but patterns of choice in privatization education evince increased stratification in school by income and race (Fleming, Cowen, Witte, and Wolf, 2013).

Tailor-made for selecting privatization education, this propensity becomes what will be referred to in this discussion as *default choice.*

Default choice constitutes a simple and certain response to the complexity and uncertainty of learning, the common good, and student-centric intentions in traditional public education. Default choice entails action to ensure that free market schooling offers predictability in self-serving comfort zones.

"As Mezirow (1997) observes, 'We have a strong tendency to reject ideas that fail to fit our preconceptions, labeling those ideas as unworthy of consideration—aberrations, nonsense, irrelevant, weird, or mistaken' (p. 5)" (Swensson, Ellis, and Shaffer, 2019b, 61).

Falling back on the simplicity of default choice for US education mirrors the tendency of human beings to "rely on automatic responses that work well for ordinary situations we see over and over" (Ludwig, 2022). This tendency—identified in research and referred to as *the Stroop test*—confirms that "conscious, deliberate thought is taxing, so our minds try to avoid it as much as possible" (Ludwig, 2022).

Form, the shape of tenets of free market theory and adult-centric intentions, provides adherents of marketplace education with non-taxing, tried and true choices that regulate or maintain themselves.

Familiar patterns are alluring and spawn automatic responses within easy reach of privatization proponents: form, accountability *to,* and responsibility given. These responses constitute the linearity of default choice for ideological purity. For marketplace adherents, default choice simplifies the struggle over US education.

INVESTING IN THE NARRATIVE OF A COMPLEX JOURNEY

Default choice facilitates the demolition of complexity and balance in public education. Demolishing complexity and balance with the free market sledgehammer of public dissonance, proponents of privatization education shatter *the public* and public things.

Attenuation, competition, and reform are preferred by marketplace proponents for "demo day." Default choice beckons legislators, citizens, and educators to demolish the enduring complexities of learning, the uncomfortable diversity of public education, and the uncertain outcomes realized when students and citizens engage with *how to think* on behalf of the common good. Familiar patterns, automatic responses, certainty, and comfort zones deter the need for conscious thought.

But comfort zones can only hide, not eliminate, the complexities, discomfort, and uncertainty that are persistent elements in the narratives of US society and traditional public education. "Indeed, it is the basic conflicts in society that make democracy essential, and it is the ability to discuss these differences in an informed and productive manner that must be a priority" (Westheimer and Kahne, 2003, 12). The difficulties and uncertainties of learning and teaching offer the setting fundamental to this level of discussion.

Public selection puts educators in position to invest in writing a narrative for the complex journey of traditional public education. This narrative equips all students with the capacities required for informed discussion that leads to balance between individual rights and functions of democracy.

The capacity of public educators to make this investment is enhanced by a guide that accommodates the complexity, discomfort, and uncertainty in learning: Gestalt of Choice.

Investing in a complicated journey, instead of a simple destination, public educators use Gestalt of Choice to plan, implement, and assess student learning. Gestalt of Choice is each public educator's self-generated access-array for student-centric instruction.

Student-Centric Instruction: Science, Art, and M. C. Escher

Teaching and learning are always complex, sometimes confusing, frequently rewarding, and often hard work. To engage all students, teaching can resemble art created by M. C. Escher.

Escher, a renowned twentieth-century graphic artist, created works in which seemingly impossible juxtapositions of shape, shading, dimension, and meaning are the norm. Among these works, *Relativity* (created in 1953) depicts figures traversing a wildly complicated array of stairs.

Navigating these stairs (metaphorically speaking) is one way to imagine Gestalt of Choice as a public educator's professional reflection and action, a creative, daunting, complex, and intricate interrelationship between art and science for student-centric instruction.

Gestalt of Choice is functionality necessary and sufficient to select learning opportunities that respond successfully to the insightful observation that "teaching is enormously demanding, frequently frustrating, occasionally overwhelming, and always an eclectic mix of planned formality and spontaneous serendipity" (Campbell, 2008, 607).

Gestalt of Choice (see Figure 9.1) guides an educator's planning, implementation, and assessment of student learning. Gestalt of Choice puts an educator in position to engage students' prior learning, meaning-making, lived experience, and intelligences in pursuit of the primary purpose of traditional US public education: *how to think* on behalf of the common good.

GESTALT OF CHOICE

Stipulated for this discussion, Gestalt of Choice is the functionality with which public educators can design and implement an ecology of learning that involves all students in a classroom. Gestalt of Choice is an educator's professional composition of a student-centric instructional narrative.

This educator-created array of practices, concepts, and information is used to imagine, then enact, connections between the universe of discourse and dynamic instruction. These connections are expressed in the instructional strategies that engage student intelligence or meaning-making with the

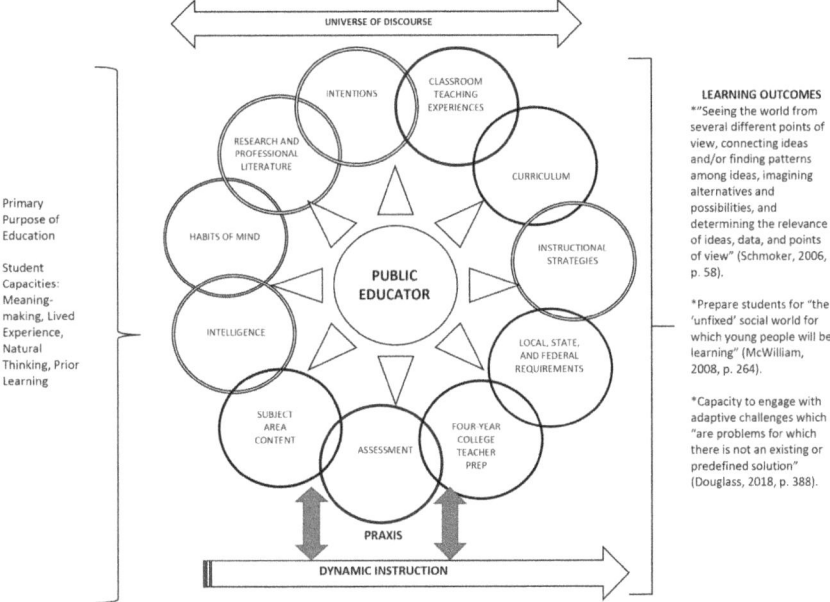

Figure 9.1 Gestalt of Choice. Author Created

original power of education. Engagement of all students with *how to think* and the common good is the sine qua non of an ecology of learning.

Selecting a Student-Centric Narrative

M. C. Escher's art gives public educators a metaphor for the complexity, variety, challenge, and uncertainty embedded in a student-centric classroom ecology. Gestalt of Choice gives public educators an array of opportunities and options required to navigate successfully during the journey of learning on behalf of the common good in traditional public education.

Each teacher articulates her/his chosen array of elements in a Gestalt of Choice. Gestalt of Choice is an educator's visualization of factors, ideas, strategies, and research available for teaching within the *universe of discourse* and *dynamic instruction.* An educator's professional judgment links various factors from a Gestalt of Choice to create learning experiences in the classroom. Gestalt of Choice is relevant to classroom pursuit of primary purpose in any grade level or subject area and promotes responsive feedback to student learning needs.

The instructional value of Gestalt of Choice lies in its student-centric suitability; flexible and context-connected, each Gestalt of Choice begins as a blank slate. The access points shown in Figure 9.1 are representative of the array created by each educator and with which the educator works within an ecology of learning.

Creating, using, and continuously improving the access points or elements in a Gestalt of Choice, a public educator accepts responsibility to evolve the learning of all students. The skills, constructs, information, professional resources, and other elements that a teacher incorporates in a Gestalt of Choice (see Figure 9.1) build the nexus for decision-making about professional behaviors and communications that lead student meaning-making.

Meaning-Making and Intelligence

Meaning-making or intelligence is the way that individuals make sense of things. Gestalt of Choice takes on added value when teachers use it to enhance, challenge, and expand meaning-making:

- Meaning-making is "a developmental measure of how individuals organize their experience, which evolves over time" (Ignelzi, 2000, 10).
- Meaning-making has been theorized along a continuum: incorporative, impulsive, imperial, interpersonal, institutional, and inter-individual (Kegan, 1980). Kegan's theory "shines a light on the conjunction of instruction with the developmental capacities and lived experience of individuals as ways to make sense of how students engage with classroom learning" (Swensson, Ellis, and Shaffer, 2019a, 26).
- "Students engage with knowledge, creativity, complex thinking skills, and emotion when educators create and deliver instruction with a profound influence on meaning-making" (Swensson and Lehman, 2021, 53).

Intelligence: Fluid and Crystallized

There are numerous research-based ideas about intelligence or meaning-making that can be written into a teacher's Gestalt of Choice. Among these, as discussed earlier, are analytical, creative, and practical intelligence. Further, Brown, Roediger, and McDaniel (2014) indicate that intelligence can be understood as *fluid* and *crystallized* as shown in Figure 12.1.

Fluid intelligence is "the ability to reason, see relationships, think abstractly, and hold information in mind while working on a problem" (Brown, Roediger, and McDaniel, 2014, 146–47). Fluid intelligence occupies the *cognitive process dimension* of intelligence where *formal operations* have been labeled as the application of intelligence to *analyze, evaluate,* and/or *create* (Bloom, 1956; Krathwohl, 2002).

An individual's knowledge about the world and an individual's mental models and procedures from prior experiences and/or learning constitute *crystallized intelligence* (Brown, Roediger, and McDaniel, 2014). Crystallized intelligence occupies the *knowledge dimension* of intelligence where *concrete operations* have been labeled as the application of intelligence to *remember, understand,* and/or *apply.* Gestalt of Choice functions

> to lead-out fluid and crystallized intelligence of all students, [because] traditional education colleagues have the responsibility for shaping classroom environments in such a way as to integrate lived experience, capabilities, and habits of mind to bring students into the array of cognitive behaviors and agency that are successful intelligence. (Swensson, Ellis, and Shaffer, 2019b, 36)

APPLYING GESTALT OF CHOICE

The functionality of Gestalt of Choice lies in each educator's choices for interaction with its array of professional resources and behaviors.

Although there is no one way to design or use Gestalt of Choice, every Gestalt of Choice embraces *form follows function.* Beginning with meaning-making for all students as the end in mind, Gestalt of Choice presents a broad field of vision from which educators write their student-centric narrative before, during, and after formal learning experiences.

Because no one Gestalt of Choice is universal, and because every Gestalt of Choice improves as educators add, modify, or delete elements, an example of Gestalt of Choice (see Textbox 9.1) "in action" is only representative of how this model works.

TEXTBOX 9.1

A Lesson Example for Elementary Students

Applying Gestalt of Choice:

- Intelligence: *Analytical* (a combination of fluid and crystallized intelligence)
- Habit of mind: *Compare/Contrast* (using prior knowledge and identifying patterns)

NOTE: "compare" and "contrast," and ideas related to these terms, are displayed for all students to use as a visual reference during this lesson.

Dynamic Instruction

Teacher explains that students will learn how to identify what is the same (compare) and what is different (contrast) when they are thinking about things or ideas.

Teacher then shows students two readily identifiable objects chosen by the teacher. For this example, say an apple and an orange.

1. *DESCRIBE:* Teacher asks students to describe each item. The student descriptions (e.g., size, shape, color, taste, cooking applications) are displayed in two columns for all to see.
2. *COMPARE:* Teacher asks students to identify what is the same in each column.
3. *CONTRAST:* Teacher, next, asks students to identify what is different in each column.

DESCRIBE	COMPARE	CONTRAST
apple///orange	apple///orange	apple///orange
	(SAME)	(DIFFERENT)

4. *ASSESSMENT:* Teacher asks students to share
   a. What does *compare* mean?
   b. What does *contrast* mean?
   c. Tell us something that is the *same* about an apple and an orange.
   d. Tell us something that is *different* about an apple and an orange.
   e. Explain how comparing and contrasting helps you think.

NEXT STEPS

A) The next lesson could compare/contrast *fact* and *opinion.*
B) The next lesson could involve subject matter content such as
   a. Compare/contrast animals.
   b. Compare/contrast plants/trees.
   c. Compare/contrast nouns . . . verbs . . . etc.
   d. Compare/contrast adult jobs.
C) The next lesson could engage students with a different habit of mind that, later, could be applied in conjunction with compare/contrast.

Habits of Mind: Gestalt of Choice "in Action"

Habits of mind are a "'common language about learning goals to facilitate communication across persons, subject matter, and grade levels'" (Krathwohl, 2002, 212). Habits of mind are shared in verb phrases (i.e., *find patterns among ideas, suppose that, render practical*) that identify the mental work involved in these thinking skills (Swensson, Ellis, and Shaffer, 2019b).

This mental work aligns with the broad cognitive landscapes of analytical, creative, and practical intelligence as shown in Table 9.1. Sternberg and Grigorenko (2004) suggest the alignment between habits of mind and categories of intelligence:

Table 9.1: Habits of Mind and Intelligence. Author Created; Swensson, Ellis, and Shaffer 2019a

(S/G) = Sternberg & Grigorenko *(BRM) = Brown, Roediger, & McDaniel*	*Analytical Intelligence*	*Creative Intelligence*	*Practical Intelligence*
Analytical Habits of Mind**	(S/G) Judge; create; compare-contrast; evaluate; critique *(BRM) Problem-solving* Other scholars***— making connections; generate; check; finding patterns among ideas; considering multiple points of view		
Creative Habits of Mind**		(S/G) Discover; invent; suppose that; predict *(BRM) Synthesize; apply existing knowledge/habits of mind to new situations* Other scholars***— activating background or *a priori* knowledge; plan; produce; imagining alternatives and possibilities	

Practical *Habits of Mind***	(S/G) Put into practice; render practical; apply; implement
	(BRM) Adapt to everyday life
	Other scholars***—observe; classify; organize; prioritize; recognize; clarifying; question-generating

(*Source: Author created; Swensson, Ellis, and Shaffer, 2019a*)

* Author's note: Habits of mind shown here are a small sample of the broad research landscape of thinking skills.

**Although habits of mind are often introduced individually through direct instruction, thinking skills, like subject areas, are powerful when utilized in combination. What amounts to an "interdisciplinary" application of habits of mind is suggested by thinking skills such as "recognizing cause-effect relationships, making analogies and generalizations, critically examining evidence, [and] using imagination to build narratives (Mezirow, 1997)" (Swensson, Ellis, and Shaffer, 2019a, 21).

***Other scholars include: Fisher and Frey, (2008); Krathwohl, (2002); Ritchart and Perkins, (2005); Schmoker, (2006)

- Habits of mind associated with analytical thinking include, *create, judge, compare/contrast, evaluate,* and *critique* (275);
- Habits of mind associated with creative thinking include, *discover, invent, suppose that,* and *predict* (275);
- Habits of mind associated with practical thinking include, *put into practice, render practical, apply,* and *implement* (275).

Gestalt of Choice and the Journey of Education

Gestalt of Choice is the evolving, educator-created, array of resources and professional behaviors (e.g., research, prior experience, instructional strategies, data, knowledge) utilized during day-to-day teaching and learning. This array fuels the exchange of intelligences in a classroom that grows and improves student meaning-making.

Gestalt of Choice permits a multitude of possible connections between the universe of discourse and *dynamic instruction*. Teachers build connections from Gestalt of Choice during instruction designed as a journey from which students acquire information, data, values of moral obligation, and habits of mind.

Nothing about teaching, learning, or the original power of education is easy or simple. Gestalt of Choice allows traditional public educators to engage with complexity and interrelate the universe of discourse for learning with professional behaviors necessary and sufficient for student-centric instruction. This dynamic instruction challenges, informs, improves, and expands meaning-making.

The frenzy for simplicity engineered by proponents of marketplace education, ironically, is an acknowledgment that US education is complex, uncomfortable, and uncertain. Default choice is offered as a cure for complexity and as a guarantor of default choices offered by adult-centric intentions for US education.

This veneer of simple intentions, however, is a masquerade: multiple interventions behind the scenes (e.g., the submerged state, attenuation, mechanisms) belie the simplicity of the marketplace. The battle over choice about educational choice is complicated further when free market proponents reinforce privatization with the particular venom within synergy of struggle: disdain.

Chapter 10

Choosing Disdain,
Engineering Decline

EMAIL
To: Traditional Public Educators
Fr: Marketeers at the Virtual Charter School
Re: School-Year Wishes for You

For proponents of free market theory, the battle with traditional public education over choice is not about learning. Rather, the struggle is over *choice about educational choice.*

The tenets of free market theory elevate the struggle between the two major perspectives beyond a kerfuffle over choice about learning. To win this competition, marketeers ensure that choice about educational choice is operationalized through *disdain* for and *decline* of traditional public education.

Threats to default choice (e.g., intentions of public education, Gestalt of Choice) constitute threats to the intended universality of free market principles. Responses to threats (e.g., public dissonance, dog-eat-dog competition) are embedded in disdain and decline.

Disdain is discussed in the upcoming chapter as the free market's bulwark against connections with *the public,* the universe of discourse, and/or achievement for all students. Contempt for traditional public education is expressed when marketeers engineer countermeasures in privatization education such as exclusive enrollment, gerrymandered funding, and attenuation.

Decline of traditional public education occurs when free market-based statutes and legislative maneuvers create both insufficient funding and increasing demands. Public schools are asked to "do more with less" while funding is siphoned away to privatization schools.

Increasing demands and decreasing funds represent the ascendency of a struggle over choice about educational choice.

Disdain and decline assail the viability of traditional public education. Fear interacts with disdain and decline to foster abandonment of "the other" so that choice about educational choice is nothing less than the disconnections and separations fostered by the purposes and outcomes of an educational marketplace.

Like Sisyphus, traditional public educators are faced with conditions (e.g., increased demands and funding shortfalls) that deter the successful completion of tasks integral to primary purpose (e.g., learning, the common good). Traditional public educators are engaged in an uphill struggle to assert student-centric intentions and to write a narrative for the history of the future of US education dedicated to *how to think* on behalf of the common good.

CHOICE IS THE BATTLEGROUND

Salvos of consumer relations launch distaste (e.g., adult-centric intentions) at traditional public education. However, labeling this assault as distaste minimizes the do-or-die response to a competitor required for success in a marketplace.

As discussed already, choice about the history of the future of traditional US public education is neither simple nor straightforward. The elaborate schemes designed to safeguard the simplicities of default choice for market-place schooling testify to the complications of teaching and learning.

The machinations of free market proponents to install privatization evince a fundamental reality: choice is the core of the struggle over what is natural to America's education.

And, the Struggle Has Little to Do with Learning

For proponents of free market theory, the battle with traditional public education over choice is not about learning. Rather, the struggle is over *choice about educational choice.*

Struggle on this level enacts (1) the *us vs. them* certainty of synergy of struggle, (2) the thrill of victory when a competitor loses, and (3) disdain for those unwilling to enact adult-centric intentions as if they constitute US education.

After all, traditional public education is perceived as a governmental entity opposed to core principles of free market thinking (e.g., survival of the fittest, limitation of government intrusion, scarcity). Opposition to the tenets of free market theory elevates the struggle between the two major perspectives beyond a kerfuffle over choice about learning.

The marketplace, by design, is ideological self-aggrandizement. To win, marketeers ensure that their struggle to enshrine choice about educational choice is conducted through *disdain* for and *decline* of traditional public education.

CHOICE ABOUT EDUCATIONAL
CHOICE AND DISDAIN

The educational marketplace bristles with disdain. Because the economic truism of limited resources and limited availability of these resources is neither the driving force behind, nor the primary purpose for, traditional public education, marketeers resort to contempt (Finn, Hentges, Petrilli, and Winkler, 2009; DeAngelis and Erickson, 2018).

Marketeers direct disdain toward entities and individuals uncommitted to the linearity of default choice.

The straight line between the tenets of free market theory and the intentions of free market education leads to efficient, simple, uncomplicated, ideologically pure schooling in the marketplace. Threats to linearity (e.g., intentions of public education, dynamic instruction) constitute threats to the proposed universality of free market principles.

The Relevance of Linearity

The linearity of default choice leads to the accumulation of marketplace principles that, as history reveals, have inconsequential effects on learning and achievement. The struggle over choice about learning becomes irrelevant to proponents of the educational marketplace.

The relevance of linearity for marketplace schooling is confirmed when default choice leads to the only acceptable destination for US education: privatization.

The struggle over choice about educational choice pivots away from learning and toward the economic principles of the free market. These principles are enforced by competition and singularity and guaranteed losers.

Exclusive enrollment, gerrymandered funding, uncritical habits of mind, and marketplace competition are all engineered to ensure that choice about educational choice separates "winners" from "losers."

Survival of the fittest, and defining the "fittest" as schools/students conforming to the intentions of default choice, render "other" schools/students worthy of disdain. The disdain due to losers in the marketplace is visited upon students deemed unworthy of access to the schooling that results from default choice. Negative sanctions legislated through *accountability to* enforce ideological disdain for these students and traditional public schools.

Disdain is the language of public dissonance. Disdain wards off ideas, practices, rules, statutes, or judicial findings that threaten ideological purity and leverages the ultimate objective of proponents of marketplace education. Contempt distances the predetermined and familiar patterns of free market schooling from learning.

Default Choice and Layers of Disdain

The exercise of default choice is the exercise of disdain. Layers of disdain in the marketplace combat the perceived failures (e.g., investment, diversity, government involvement, inclusion) of traditional public education.

Instead of a journey to improved achievement and greater democracy, default choice leads to a destination where inequity, losing, and singularity represent disdain for diversity, achievement, and public things.

Disdain for diversity is expressed when default choice distances excluded cohorts of US students from enrollment in privatization education. Forms of attenuation—separation and discrimination—levy exorbitant costs on students deemed unworthy of participation in the marketplace.

Disdain has an impact on teaching and learning. Disdain for achievement inspires academic cocooning. Comfort zones encase teaching and learning in low-cost standardized instruction and the demise of assessment. Marketplace simplicity at its finest.

Marketplace restrictions on *how to think* are the ultimate contempt for student capacities and the primary purpose of traditional public education.

Disdain, further, elevates distaste for public things to a level required for dedication to the marketplace instead of *the public* and public works (Knight Abowitz and Stitzlein, 2018). Disdain for the common good, *the public, and the intelligence of all students infests the priorities of the educational marketplace. Disdain for traditional* US public education and its purpose, thus, is the fulcrum on which the future of the struggle over choice about educational choice pivots.

CHOICE ABOUT EDUCATIONAL
CHOICE AND DECLINE

Scholarship devoted to the study of organizational theory indicates that a substantial drop in the resource base of an organization over an identified time frame is decline or atrophy of the organization (McKinley, Latham, and Braun, 2014, 90).

The decline of traditional public education occurs when the principles of free market theory lead to insufficient funding for public schooling and/or reallocation of tax dollars to privatization education. At the same time default choice fosters decline through insufficient funding, increased demands are placed on traditional public educators:

- While public dissonance reduces funding for traditional public education, community services are pawned off on traditional public schools. "Rather than relying simply on school-based action to help students thrive, efforts to address matters such as poverty, health, and safety in the neighborhoods and communities where students live are increasingly included in education initiatives" (Miller, Scanlan, and Wills, 2014, 1).
- Reduced funding for civic organizations—established in alignment with free market thinking—puts public schools in a position where overwhelming demands exacerbate the insufficiencies inherent in educational adequacy defined as minimum quality.
- Increased numbers of privatization schools and enrolled students mean that resources dwindle for traditional US public schools (Rich, 2014).
- Vouchers, legislative largesse, and/or tax credit "scholarships" are among the free market devices that generate turbulence and siphon funds away from traditional public education (Hefling, 2017).
- As described by Nutt (2004) organizational atrophy is signaled by "perverse incentives, differentiation without integration, role confusion, decentralization with shifting mandates, rigid and inappropriate rules, stifled dissent, victim blaming, and obsolescence grow" (1087). These characteristics grow throughout traditional public education when attenuation, public dissonance, and disdain replace the struggle over choice about learning with a struggle over choice about educational choice. Prioritizing a struggle over choice about educational choice is the road to a winner-take-all future.

Default choice advances free market priorities whose purpose is to turn public education competitors into losers. When student-centric education loses, to the victor go the spoils.

Choice "Wins," Funding "Loses"

Choice about educational choice in the twenty-first century is described as a "political competition between two competing advocacy networks and coalitions that want to expand or constrain school choice" (Reckhow, Grossman, and Evans, 2015, 208).

Some of the evidence that political competition entails marketplace consequences is found in research that indicates that:

- A total of forty-two states, between 2009–2010 and 2016–2017, "decreased their average annual salary for public school teachers" (Rentner, 2019, 4).
- In the wake of the Great Recession, "there are still 170,000 fewer jobs in public education than there were before the recession, despite public school enrollment being 1.5 million higher" (AFT, 2018).
- During the first sixteen years of the twenty-first century, "the nation's per-pupil expenditure (adjusted for inflation) in public schools increased by barely more than 14 percent—less than half the rate of growth in the numbers of poor students" (Suitts, 2016, 37).

But, a description and data that suggests that choice about educational choice is political, glosses over the ultimate objective of marketplace adherents: the obliteration of competition, aka traditional public education (Chubb and Moe, 1990; Mead, 2016; Wolf, et al., 2014). Disdain is the platform from which marketplace adherents launch the ultimate weapon in the struggle over choice about educational choice: decline. Decline, of course, depends on reducing resources for public education.

During the latter part of the twentieth century and the early decades of the twenty-first century, "the rhetoric of choice eventually replaced adequate resources" (Gunzenhauser and Hyde, 2007, 497) in the struggle between the major perspectives for supremacy over and control of the narrative for the history of the future of US education.

The groundwork for this shift to a struggle over choice of educational choice was prepared earlier when adequacy was defined as a minimum while, simultaneously, educational gerrymandering delivered funding insufficiencies. The rhetoric of choice, espoused with gusto by marketeers, supplanted the debate about educational resources sufficient to establish academic success for all US students.

Rhetoric designed to defend and implement default choice is conveyed in statutory bulwarks, fiscal chicanery, and/or rejection of *the public*. Increasing demands and decreasing funds that accompany the ascendency of struggle over choice about educational choice assail the viability of traditional public education and the future of learning.

DISDAIN: DECLINE OF THE "OTHER"

The educational marketplace is intentionally inhospitable. Tenets of free market theory limit "winners." "Others" are not welcome in the educational marketplace except as "losers." Winners in this environment have nothing but disdain for losers.

The ethos of competition and the intense focus on winning in the marketplace emerges from an unrelenting focus on scarcity. Scarce resources and identification of "winners" who "deserve" these resources occupy the time and talents of marketplace adherents.

Disconnecting losers from resources is part of competition. Thus, proponents of marketplace education want little to do with connecting learning on behalf of the common good with sufficient resources.

The relationship between democracy and citizenship education, for example, depends upon connection between dynamic instruction and the values of moral obligation incorporated via Gestalt of Choice in the ecology of a classroom. These characteristics of a public thing are costly complexities laden with uncertainties because "others" (e.g., all US students) are prioritized. A simple choice about educational choice avoids connection and assures efficiency.

Linearity vs. Complexity of "Others"

Default choice is "linearity [that] rivets high minimum quality to the blinders of singularity. The result is that contemporary declarations about a good school tend to be self-fulfilling prophecies that equate adequacy or purpose of public education with self-interest (Roda and Wells, 2013)" (Swensson and Shaffer, 2020, 53).

Linearity, the efficiency of default choice, is the one-way street to the marketplace. Efficiency, in this case, is an example of choice to deny sufficient resources to traditional public education. Efficiency, in this case, is an example of choice to increase the demands on public education (i.e., "do more with less").

Trapped in this cycle, traditional public education declines and *the public* is denied a role in the public sector. "Others" are fit to play the role in the educational marketplace designated for them by the principles of free market theory. Disdain for those excluded from winning in the marketplace is fear-induced.

FEAR: DISDAIN FOR "LOSERS"

"Others" are not linear. "Others" are *the public, complex to the point of fore-stalling default choice for* US education. Free market theory, buttressed by my-side bias and the synergy of struggle, designates the complexity and cost of "others" as a threat to the limitations visited upon public life by market-place education.

Singularity is a marketplace priority. So is competition. But, competition can result in losing, which is not a marketplace priority. Moreover, losing during competition implies the possibility that "others" might emerge as "winners."

For marketeers, singularity preserves winning. Disdain preserves the simplicity of singularity in the marketplace. Default choice erases complexity and prioritizes the "right" to singularity in pursuit of winning that guarantees that "the other" is a loser.

Above all, losing is a fearful proposition for marketeers. Fear of losing accentuates the value of contempt for losers, aka competitors, aka traditional public educators. Disdain wards off fear and enhances the self-serving righteousness that flourishes as synergy of struggle. Free market fears are expressed in many forms of contempt:

- *Disdain for government.* Fear of government "intrusion" in any aspect of life suffuses free market theory. From this point of view, traditional public education, aka "government schools," curtails individual rights. Fear that government exists to prevent or take away individual freedom legitimizes the need to battle over choice of educational choice. Singularity, *accountability to* free market theory, and cost avoidance deconstruct connections and mutuality that constitute the role of "government schools" in the public sector.
- *Disdain for the public.* There is no guarantee that *the public* will prioritize free market education. An aggregation like *the public* is fear-inducing in that it does not prioritize singularity. Contemptable characteristics of public things, public life, and public work like democracy, desegregation, diversity, and equity abrogate this marketplace priority. Disdain for *the public* supports the every-person-is-an-island ethos of singularity.
- *Disdain for connection.* Singularity is "winning" aided and abetted by attenuation and the submerged state. Connection is contemptible because it undermines self-aggrandizing behaviors and goals. Disdain for interrelationships, new knowledge, *how to think*, the common good, and other connections reinforces the disconnections that distance fear from the marketplace.

Selling "Fear Itself"

Marketplace education, guided by disdain and decline, is the route to solutions that deliver ideological certainty. Fear of losing, fear of market failure, fear of "others," fear of connection—all are sales campaigns in the marketplace.

Fear is compelling. Fear is resistant to logic, fact, and evidence. Statements that induce fear do so efficiently and with little regard for accuracy. As Stanley Kurtz proclaimed about instruction in traditional public education, "'we should not be barring the discussion or understanding of concepts, only the teaching of them as truths to be embraced'" (Powell, 2021).

Fear is its own layer of disdain and pushes aside evidence that traditional public educators do not teach "truths to be embraced." Free market proponents inveigh against the perceived threats (e.g., inconvenient lessons) in traditional public education and fear justifies a resort to quick, efficient, solutions.

The power of fear is maximized when, to paraphrase President Franklin D. Roosevelt, the marketplace manufactures fear of fear itself. Fear that supports singularity, fear that validates public dissonance, and fear that promotes restrictions is directed at parents and caregivers.

Lurid claims about traditional public education—one politician "took aim at school library shelves, directing education officials to investigate 'criminal activity in our public schools involving the availability of pornography'" (Powell, 2021)—stoke fear about government "intrusion" and about *the public's* intentions for children. Fear becomes its own justification; truth and accuracy are trampled when the history of the future of US public education is a narrative of choice about educational choice.

Malicious attacks on traditional public education and its purpose represent an expression of fear dedicated to education for the self-interest of what to think. Marketplace schooling, as a result, features:

- Singularity and the disdain expressed in *uncritical habits of mind.* Contempt for students' racial, ethnic, religious, and/or language-lived experience infests laissez-faire marketplace schooling (Suitts, 2016; 2019). A "free" market for education where oversight is lax and in which the ethos is dog-eat-dog gives permission to discriminate.
- Standardized instruction validates preconceived notions, proclivities, and prejudices about what is and what is not a learnable moment. What-to-think becomes a priority. *Status quo ante educere* (as things were before leading-out) describes the retrograde motion of marketplace education that limits meaning-making to conformance with principles of ideological purity and the restrictions of natural thinking.

• Citizenship education falters when disdain and its characteristics (e.g., singularity, discrimination, segregation) become a baseline for disconnection. As Laguardia and Pearl (2009) observe, "the mad dash to add obstacles (standards) and centralized control (accountability) destroys the hard won vestiges of democracy in education and by so doing seriously undermines the societal democracy that has been hard won over the past two centuries" (353).

SELF-INTEREST DISDAINS "OTHERS"

The educational marketplace is where "others" are an obstacle to self-interest. My-side bias and linearity render self-interest infused with fear socially valuable.

"Others" and self-interest are rendered, in this way, incompatible. Self-interest dictates exclusion of "the other" because "the other" is competition in the marketplace. By excluding "the other" resources are earmarked for the exclusive use of winners. When self-interest embedded in the ethos of marketplace schooling is threatened, fear—of losing resources, profit, and/or ideological purity; of "the other"—takes hold.

Up and Down the Hill with Sisyphus

The eternal fate of Sisyphus, a mythic character from Roman times, is instructive during any consideration of the history of the future of public education. His task was to push a boulder to the top of a hill. Each time Sisyphus inched the boulder close to the summit, it rolled back to the bottom of the hill, where, once again, Sisyphus was compelled to push his boulder.

Like Sisyphus, traditional public educators are faced with conditions (e.g., increased demands and funding shortfalls) that deter the successful completion of difficult tasks integral to primary purpose (e.g., learning, the common good). These circumstances have a dire effect on traditional public schools as organizations (Weitzel and Jonsson, 1989).

Organizational atrophy of traditional public education is compounded by the disappearing connections between US families and civic, religious, and governmental entities. Just as teaching and learning are impeded by adult-centric intentions, public schools are weighed down by social tasks assigned by fear-mongering statutes or that other organizations have jettisoned.

Traditional public educators are engaged in an uphill struggle to assert student-centric intentions and to write a narrative for the history of the future of US education dedicated to *how to think* on behalf of the common good.

Instead of accepting a Sisyphus-like assignment from proponents of free market theory, however, traditional public educators can access professional skills that create an ecology of learning and the dynamic instruction necessary and sufficient for the student-centric education that all students and US democracy deserve.

Chapter 11

Reciprocity Is Public Education

EMAIL
To: Traditional Public Educators
Fr: Your Colleague Down the Hall
Re: Classroom Ecologies, Reciprocity, and Learning

Begin with the end in mind. This tried-and-true aphorism is just one characteristic of traditional public education that speaks to the interrelationship between classroom ecologies, reciprocity, teaching, and learning.

In the upcoming chapter, reciprocity is explored as the essential interaction between intelligences that defines the ecology in a classroom. Meaning-making emerges from this relationship; students acquire creative, practical, and academic skills to flourish individually and as citizens in US democracy.

Meaning-making in the ecology of a classroom is essential for the reciprocity of balance. The intricacies of balance are depicted by "Sternberg, Reznitskaya, and Jarvin (2007) who observe that 'wise thinking involves the ability to use one's intelligence in the service of a common good by balancing one's own interests with those of other people and of a broader community over both the short- and long-terms' (p. 150)" (Swensson, Ellis, and Shaffer, 2019b, 19).

Understanding the role of reciprocity within the ecologies of learning and the classroom, public educators bring the original power of education to fruition. The transformation of meaning-making created when public educators begin with the end in mind directs how choice will affect America's future.

In the upcoming chapter, public value creation is discussed as an outcome of choice that depends on form follows function. Connecting the purpose of traditional public education with Gestalt of Choice, public educators ensure that student-centric intentions and dynamic instruction are essential elements of public value creation.

Although no magic wand can be waved so the narrative about the history of the future of public education expresses student-centric intentions, public educators whose professional choices foster reciprocity utilize instrumental agency to render connections, balance, and the ecology of learning socially valuable.

THE ECOLOGIES OF TRADITIONAL PUBLIC EDUCATION

Although unique in many ways, all classrooms share a similarity derived from Bronfenbrenner's (1979) ecological systems theory: Everything in a classroom is related in one way or another. Ecological systems theory "is presented as a theory of human development in which everything is seen as interrelated and our knowledge of development is bounded by context, culture, and history" (Darling, 2007, 204).

Traditional public education is a choice to engage all students in the ecology of a classroom with meaning-making necessary and sufficient to understand, reflect upon, and take principled action about the interrelations and connections that develop in their lives.

Developing the intelligences of all students in the ecology of a classroom, public educators employ context, culture, and history in a narrative about learning written via Gestalt of Choice, dynamic instruction, and the values of moral obligation.

Meaning-making in the ecology of the classroom engages the intelligences of all students with the universe of discourse. Meaning-making becomes a reciprocal engagement; students acquire creative, practical, and academic skills to flourish individually and as citizens in US democracy. Meaning-making grows, under these conditions, beyond singularity to intelligence that balances the common good with individuality.

Balance reflects the enduring reciprocity at the heart of US public education. Balance is the result of the relationship between traditional public schooling and citizenship. At the foundation of this relationship is the understanding that "citizens share a stated or implicit covenant with the state" (Stitzlein, 2015, 575).

A Student-Centric Ecology

Give-and-take, starting over, collaboration, starting from scratch, moving beyond prior learning—all represent the reciprocity in meaning-making. The ecology of learning and the ecology of the classroom are investments in reciprocity.

Everything public educators do, either directly or indirectly, is related to the exchanges—between ideas, information, prior learning, hypotheses—animated by Gestalt of Choice for dynamic instruction during student learning.

Growth of a student's meaning-making in this ecology (an educator's professional judgement about student capacities for *how to think* on behalf of the common good) is assessed via several indicators, including:

- The extent to which students demonstrate age-appropriate and prior-learning-based understanding that "it is not enough to simply consume predigested knowledge, one must also become a knowledge builder (Scandamalia, Bereiter, and Lamon, 1994) and problem solver (Polya, 1957; Schoenfeld, 1982; Selz, 1935)" (Ritchart and Perkins, 2005, 777).
- The extent to which students demonstrate age-appropriate and prior-learning-based evidence of "the special human capacity for 'theory of mind' [which] allows us to appreciate that we may have different perspectives and concerns" (Mercer, 2013, 163).
- The extent to which students demonstrate capacities for connecting elements from the universe of discourse that prompt principled action. And the extent to which students demonstrate capacities for justifying connections in terms of *how to think* and the values of the moral obligation of traditional public education.

A Focus on Learning as Connections

Learning develops when public educators engage all students with meaning-making from connections and interrelationships between the universe of discourse and dynamic instruction. Gestalt of Choice is the lens necessary and sufficient to focus professional choices on the connections and interrelationships for learning available every day in the analytic, creative, and practical reciprocities of meaning-making.

Understanding the role of reciprocity within the ecologies of learning and the classroom, public educators bring a focus on the original power of education to fruition. The reciprocal relationship between *how to think* and the moral obligation of public education shapes the ecologies of a public school classroom in which:

- Public educators "repeatedly rise to the occasion—adopting a sustained, experimental, and pluralistic approach that supports full and diverse expressions of openness, humility, collaboration, and willingness to grapple with uncertainty and ambiguity (Ansell 2011; Biesta 2009; Campbell 2008; Hytten 2009)" (Kurth-Schai, 2014, 428).

- Meaning-making in the ecology of a classroom is essential for the reciprocity of balance. The intricacies of balance are depicted by "Sternberg, Reznitskaya, and Jarvin (2007) who observe that 'wise thinking involves the ability to use one's intelligence in the service of a common good by balancing one's own interests with those of other people and of a broader community over both the short- and long-terms' (p. 150)" (Swensson, Ellis, and Shaffer, 2019b, 19).
- The original power of education facilitates reciprocity between individuals and *the public* as balance "connected by common concerns about their shared fate, care for the interests of others, and the desire to seek shared principles that enable them to work out differences" (Stitzlein, 2015, 566).

Four principles relevant to ecological systems theory—interdependence, open systems and feedback loops, cycling of resources, and adaptation (Wielkiewicz and Stelzner, 2005, 326–27)—suffuse the ecology of learning and the ecology of any classroom. For instance, Gestalt of Choice and dynamic instruction are interdependent open systems that facilitate feedback loops throughout teaching and learning.

The Social Value of Ecologies

The ecology of a traditional public school classroom empowers all students to acquire and work with capacities necessary and sufficient to tackle ambiguities, uncertainty, and the multitude of life circumstances that lie in their futures. These capacities constitute engagement in *the public*.

The ecology of learning in America's public schools embraces an obligation to citizenship in US democracy. This commitment is both an investment in and the cost of "the underlying importance of reinforcing good moral values that transcend normative social or cultural differences among us and instead nurture a positive sense of our collective humanity" (Campbell, 2008, 609).

How to think is socially valuable in this context because democracy requires citizens capable of reciprocity for balance within interrelationships that are *the public*.

The values of moral obligation are the foundation for the reciprocity between democracy and learning. A future in which all students fulfill the obligations of citizenship in democracy develops from "the fundamental moral purpose of deep and broad learning (Hargreaves and Fink, 2006, p. 27)" (Leo and Wickenberg, 2013, 412).

Public Value Creation

How to think on behalf of the common good nurtures a positive sense for collective humanity and represents *public value creation*.

"Public value creation is defined as 'producing what is either valued by the public, is good for the public, including adding to the public sphere, or both, as assessed against various public value criteria' (Bryson, Crosby, and Bloomberg, 2014, p. 448)" (Merritt, Kennedy, and Farnworth, 2020, 154). But, considering the marketplace priorities and outcomes discussed thus far, caution is in order.

If something is valued by the public, but not assessed against public value criteria that incorporate the values of moral obligation and is not sufficient for balance, then public value creation is little more than a monument to ideological self-interest.

Disdain for balance between individual needs and the interests of *the public* is the baseline from which the tenets of free market theory disdain reciprocity. Contempt for balance creates a singularity-driven ecology in which *accountability to* free market theory is the only socially valuable thing.

Meaning-making in the marketplace is hemmed in by adult-centric intentions and the ideological guardrails that disconnect learning from the universe of discourse. Proponents of free market schooling promote a restrictive ecology in which "they more highly value individual freedoms and the desire to pursue them, either independently or alongside like-minded others, without seeking to establish a clear community" (Stitzlein, 2015, 576).

Reciprocity within and between the values of moral obligation and *how to think*, as discussed earlier, facilitates reflection and action from which a balance between public requirements and individual interests eventuates. Balance in democracy is not only a socially valuable outcome of traditional public education but also a benchmark with which to assess public value creation.

RECIPROCITY, BALANCE, AND THE
TRANSFORMATION OF MEANING-MAKING

As this discussion noted earlier, all human beings make sense of things initially via natural thinking within their lived experience.

Meaning-making through natural thinking alone is insufficient, however, to make sense of the burgeoning interconnections, interrelationships, contexts, cultures, and histories that students encounter as they grow up.

Recognizing this, public educators "prepare the environment and facilitate the relationships necessary to support diverse learners as they experience social inquiry, discover shared purpose, and translate collective goals into principled action" (Kurth-Schai, 2014, 432).

Wise thinking and successful intelligence represent the reciprocities in meaning-making facilitated when Gestalt of Choice empowers a range of professional behaviors that yield learning outcomes. When public educators engage students with knowledge-building and problem-solving via dynamic instruction, connections multiply and capacities for balance grow.

Gestalt of Choice, a whole that is more than the sum of its parts, facilitates an ecology in which interrelationship and connections are natural to public education. Persistent intellectual exchange and reciprocity expressed in the original power of education engage all students with capacities for balance, wisdom, positive liberty, and public life in US democracy.

HOW TO WRITE THE FUTURE; HOW TO MAKE A CHOICE

Traditional public educators have a great deal of leverage when it comes to choosing the narrative for the future of US schooling.

Leverage comes from the fact that 90 percent of America's students are enrolled in public schools. Leverage comes from the fact that heavy majorities of parents and caregivers value and appreciate the traditional public school where their child(ren) attends. Leverage comes from the fact that university-trained graduates of four-year college programs enter the profession equipped to create and access Gestalt of Choice to engage student intelligences with the universe of discourse and dynamic instruction.

As this discussion reveals, however, multiple forces and factors stand in the way of a student-centric narrative for the history of the future of US education. Choice about perspective and intentions is entangled with legislatures, statutes, foundations, PACs (political action committees), community groups, and a host of other actors who enter the fray to determine how US education should play its role in the public sector.

None of these actors and none of their intentions deserve to be prioritized ahead of the purpose for public education that all students deserve: prioritize student learning on behalf of the nation's democracy. This means that inconvenient lessons identified by proponents of free market schooling constitute a substantial deviation from a future narrative for education that benefits all students.

Public educators are in possession of a significant resource that contributes effectively to this storyline: *dynamic instruction.*

Dynamic instruction, discussed in the upcoming chapter, is a public educator's commitment to learning and the futures of all students that depend on learning. The professional responsibility for something greater than self is dedicated to engaging all students in the balance intended in the ecology of learning fostered by traditional public educators.

Connecting with the future of traditional US public education is more than a choice about educational choice. To base teaching and learning on the unyielding and unresponsive tenets of a marketplace welded to adult-centric intentions is the abandonment of learning and the limitation of society to a predetermined "educated" few.

An ecology of learning in which everything is connected and from which learning is meaning-making that makes sense of connections cannot develop from intentional restrictions and the denial of learning for all US students.

Because democracy—an immensely complicated ecology—requires from public education a commitment to "social integration and the good of others" (Stitzlein, 2015, 575), dynamic instruction is the instrumental agency of public education professionals necessary and sufficient for schools to balance individual futures alongside effective citizenship.

Traditional public education offers an open door to *how to think* for all students. Traditional public educators, thus, control the essential resource required to narrate the history of the future of US public education devoted to societal and individual success.

Chapter 12

A Resource and a Professional Capability

Dynamic Instruction

EMAIL
To: Traditional Public Educators
Fr: Instructional Coaches
Re: Choosing a Student-Centric Narrative

The battle to control the narrative for the history of the future of America's education is underway. Contemporary US educators struggle over two major perspectives. One perspective writes an adult-centric narrative. The other perspective writes a student-centric narrative.

Proponents of the adult-centric narrative present a simple prose dedicated to the linearity of schooling outcomes derived from free market theory. Proponents of the student-centric narrative present a complex, intricate, prose dedicated to engaging learners with *how to think* on behalf of the common good.

One factor will determine which of these two narratives tells the future tale of public education: *dynamic instruction*.

Dynamic instruction engages all students with the original power of education. Dynamic instruction fosters the balance of US democracy; the capacities of intelligences that confront unknowns, ambiguities, and public dissonance; and the wherewithal for continuous improvement. Dynamic instruction in the ecology of the classroom is the pivot point from which traditional public educators can write the future narrative that all US students deserve.

Proponents of standardized instruction, conversely, employ the tenets of free market theory to restrict, limit, and deny the original power of education. Cookie-cutter instructional strategies used in the educational marketplace restrict access to "uncomfortable" ideas and limit expressions and development of wisdom.

Instead of limitation, the instrumental agency of each public educator is the capacity to generate teaching that opens cognitive doors for all students. *Direct instruction, active learning, and assessment* are among the foundational teaching behaviors discussed in this chapter.

Accessing Gestalt of Choice, public educators select among an array of options for active learning. During dynamic instruction, students use habits of mind, ideas, information, and/or data to develop meaning-making and make sense out of adaptive challenges, creative opportunities, and/or practical dilemmas.

The meaning-making fostered when students participate in these interrelations of an *ecology of learning* is explored as the essential justification for teaching and learning dedicated to student-centric outcomes.

A COMPLEX CHAIN OF EVENTS

Accountable for all students, and accepting responsibility for things greater than self, educators pursue the purpose of traditional public education by engaging in the "'complex chain of events'" (Gunzenhauser and Hyde, 2007, 503) referred to as instruction or teaching.

The ecology of a classroom requires teaching, reflection and action of professional public educators, necessary and sufficient to grow and challenge the meaning-making of all students.

Complex pedagogy—referred to in this discussion as *dynamic instruction*—incorporates public selection, Gestalt of Choice, accountability *for* all students, and acceptance of responsibility.

Always in the Way of Student-Centric Learning

Standing in the way of dynamic instruction and a student-centric education, standardized instruction, materials, and testing are barriers that separate *how to think* from the learning experiences of students. Segregated and restrictive, the virtual, voucher, and other privatization entities funded through the auspices of state government impede both teaching and learning for all US students.

Distance and disdain "protect" students from the original power of education. Free market theory, default choice, accountability *to*, and singularity are among the ideological imperatives embedded in standardized instruction offered in the marketplace.

The Bitter, Adult-Centric, Struggle Over Learning

From the perspective of proponents of free market schooling, learning is unnecessarily inefficient and costly. Critics of traditional US public education turn to standardized instruction (e.g., computer-assisted learning, unlicensed teachers, large class size, virtual education) to ward off complexity and inefficiency while, at the same time, delivering fiscal insufficiencies to traditional public education and profit to marketeers.

Many of these attempts are reminiscent of the historic effort to create *teacher-proof* materials that, in the twenty-first century, have metastasized into statutory bans against topics and literature (Powell, 2022). Conformity to limitations imposed by free market ideology standardizes instruction.

These restrictions constrain the universe of discourse and supersede the values of moral obligation. Prepackaged learning is delivered via free market thinking in such a way as to ration or preclude *how to think.*

Textbook content is manipulated to delete complexity and/or the uncertainties of concepts or ideas deemed ideologically objectionable. Standardized instruction is default choice by another name. Standardized instruction ensures that the exchange of intelligences between educators and students is truncated.

CHOICE, INSTRUCTION, AND CONTROL

Either public selection for traditional public education, or default choice for privatization education: these are the choices that point the way to teaching and learning in the future narrative for US education.

Default choice yields an adult-centric narrative to restrict the purpose, practice, and outcomes of instruction. Singularity, competition, and fear are baselines from which statutes forbid instruction that makes students feel "discomfort" (Herron, 2022a, 23A).

Statutory limitations on teaching and learning allow simple choices that manufacture certainty, comfort zones, and/or ideological purity to control the uncertainties (e.g., questions, unknowns, controversial topics) omnipresent in learning.

Ideological instructional materials (e.g., sectarian teaching materials) and reduced teacher-student interaction (e.g., computer-based instruction, virtual schooling, worksheets) ensure that instruction conforms to expectations of simplicity and limitation (Klein, 2017).

The alternate reality foisted on instruction under these circumstances is reinforced by cognitive guardrails erected when standardized testing sustains educational inadequacy and restricts instruction to alignment with free market outcomes.

When Choice Is More than Choice

Public selection, on the other hand, is the persistent engagement of traditional public educators with the composition of complex chains of events that equip all students with the analytic, creative, and practical capacities for the futures they deserve while securing these futures with balance in America's democracy.

Choice, it turns out, is much more than educational choice when it comes to the lives and futures of all US students. Choice about educational choice confronts teaching and learning with a dead end.

But, choice about learning permits teaching and learning to grow to meet the needs of individuals in balance with the requirements of democracy. The history of the future of traditional US public education, as it turns out, *does involve* a struggle over choice about learning. At the heart of a student-centric narrative is the instrumental agency of professional public educators referred to here as *dynamic instruction.*

Dynamic instruction in traditional public education engages all students with information, habits of mind, concepts, and data during active learning to acquire skills necessary (1) to make sense of the "unfixed" nature of the world, (2) to enact positive liberty, and (3) to seek balance between the common good and individual rights.

Dynamic instruction, further, expands meaning-making for learners. This level of control has been referred to as "release of responsibility" (Fisher and Frey, 2021) and will be referred to here as "increase of responsibility." Both phrases register the intention of dynamic instruction to engage all students with accepting greater responsibility for analytical, creative, and practical intelligence and dispositions. This intention animates the ecology of learning fostered by dynamic instruction.

DYNAMIC INSTRUCTION

Stipulated for this discussion, dynamic instruction is teaching that engages student meaning-making with *how to think* and the common good (see Figure 12.1). Dynamic instruction is an educator's instrumental agency for *educere*, accepting responsibility to lead-out the intelligence of all students.

Dynamic instruction engages the capacities that students bring to each classroom ecology to grow and express virtue (arête). Ethics and competence

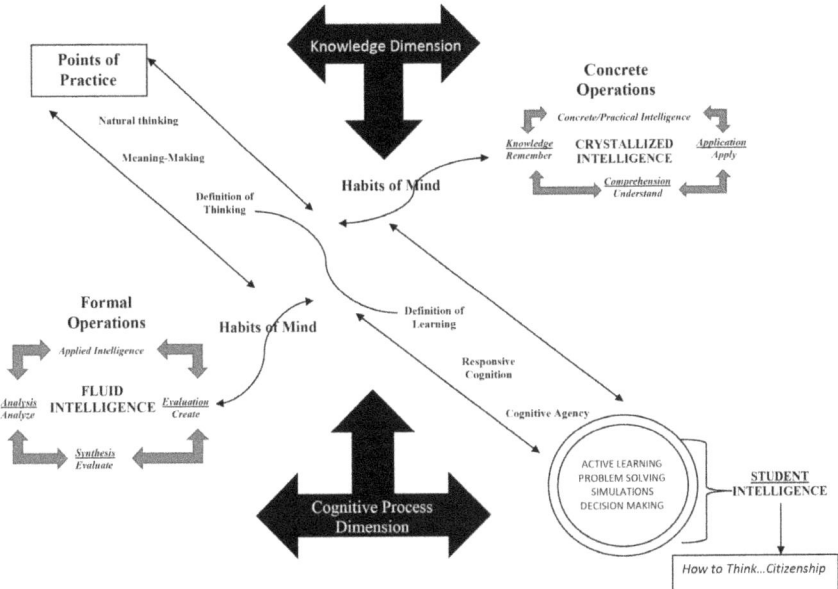

Figure 12.1 Dynamic Instruction. Author Created: Adapted from Bloom, 1956; Krathwohl, 2002; Swensson, Ellis, and Shaffer, 2019bEvery Day Educational Complexity

in meaning-making are connected via dynamic instruction with the values of the moral obligation of traditional public education.

"Day-to-day fulfillment of a sense of justice during teaching and learning typically occurs in the form of 'generalized moral and ethical values relating to how human beings should treat one another (e.g., kindly, fairly, truthfully)'" (Campbell, 2008, 608).

Dynamic instruction is a public selection of balance within students' future expressions of citizenship in US democracy.

The complexity of instruction is a daily opportunity and challenge. The complexity of dynamic instruction is the planned, flexible, serendipitous, and goal-oriented exchange of intelligences.

Dynamic instruction enlists the planned and responsive-nexus provided via Gestalt of Choice to align classroom ecologies with student-centric intentions. "'Every day, teachers call audibles at the line of scrimmage, figuring out what materials and words will work'" (Powell, 2021, 9). Gestalt of Choice represents the planned and responsive nexus required to figure out what works for learning by all students.

Dynamic instruction, as shown in Figure 12.1, is composed of a "highly complex sets of skills, intellectual functioning and knowledge that are not easily acquired and not widely held" (Ingersoll and Collins, 2017, 90).

Banks (1973), Bloom (1956), Brown, Roediger, and McDaniel (2014), Brozo and Simpson (2003), Fisher and Frey (2021), Hunter (1982), and Taba (1962) are among the scholars who provide public educators with research (accessed in the universe of discourse through Gestalt of Choice) to construct dynamic instruction.

Dynamic Instruction: Professional Skills

Public educators acquire professional skills suitable for access via Gestalt of Choice during four-year collegiate teacher education programs. Some of the strategies in this professional baseline that initiate an educator's use of dynamic instruction can be:

- *Direct instruction:* Direct instruction from a licensed teacher shares ideas, provides information, demonstrates habits of mind, and/or gives details about *how to think.* Direct instruction puts students in position to reflect upon—through discussion, questioning, and guided practice—content from the universe of discourse selected via Gestalt of Choice.
- *Guided practice:* Guided practice is an opportunity for students to "try out" the ideas, habits of mind, information, and data conveyed during direct instruction. Teachers monitor and re-teach during guided instruction to further engage students and to assess the extent to which the goals of direct instruction are realized.
- *Authentic learning:* Authentic learning puts the cognitive engagement of students "in motion" during simulations, debates, problem-solving, or other active learning scenarios. Authentic learning gives students opportunities to "test drive" the content learned during direct instruction and reinforced via guided practice. Authentic learning also provides opportunities to remember and connect with previously taught skills, concepts, and ideas.
- *Independent practice:* Independent practice (often during authentic learning experiences) is the opportunity for students to "solo" as they engage with and share what they have learned during direct instruction and guided practice. During independent practice, public educators redirect, encourage, and challenge as students apply classroom learning to active and authentic learning scenarios.
- *Emergence:* Emergence is an example of *leadership of instruction* (Swensson and Lehman, 2021). "Emergence is defined as properties of a system that 'arise from the interactions and relationships among the parts' (Capra, 1996, p. 29)" (Wielkiewicz and Stelzner, 2005, 330). Dynamic instruction leads-out student intelligence when educators enact the interrelationships between the universe of discourse, dynamic

instruction, and professional practices arrayed throughout Gestalt of Choice. Emergence describes the professional educator's use of Gestalt of Choice to create interactions and relationships essential to the expansion of meaning-making for all students.

- *Assessment:* Formative, ongoing, assessment during dynamic instruction gives a public educator insight into the extent to which students acquire the elements of reflection and cognitive action shared during a lesson or unit of study. Dynamic instruction incorporates Gestalt of Choice to access and interconnect professional strategies and to adjust in-class communication, initiate re-teaching or acceleration, and lead-out new learning.

DYNAMIC INSTRUCTION: AN EXAMPLE

Dynamic instruction, as shown in Figure 12.1, is teaching that "gives students opportunities to build cognitive interplay and takes advantage of the brain's capacity for establishing new connections for new knowledge" (Brown, Roediger, and McDaniel, 2014; Swensson, Ellis, and Shaffer, 2019b, 37).

Dynamic instruction is an educator's interplay of professional resources and behaviors (accessed in the reciprocity between the universe of discourse and Gestalt of Choice) in a classroom ecology to sustain, challenge, and extend student intelligence. Dynamic instruction, an amalgam of interrelationships between concepts, professional behaviors, and research choreographed via Gestalt of Choice, establishes an ecology of learning.

Dynamic Instruction "At Work"

An example of dynamic instruction ("at work" in an eighth grade American history class) is featured in Textbox 12.1.

Some of the elements in this example of dynamic instruction "at work" include:

- *Intelligence & Habits of Mind:* In this lesson, students "remember" (see Figure 12.1, *Concrete Operations/Crystallized* Intelligence) by accessing prior learning about causes of the Civil War. To access memory about causes of the Civil War, students use "recall" strategies taught previously. (Students are asked to summarize these "recall" strategies at the beginning of this lesson. This review and discussion about strategies for remembering is intended to reassure students that they have the capacity to succeed during this lesson.)

A Lesson Example for Middle School Students

Chosen from Gestalt of Choice:

- Intelligence: Concrete Operations = *remember*
- Habit of Mind
- Content: Eighth grade American history, Causes of the Civil War

Dynamic Instruction

Previous lessons have explained and students have practiced various strategies for accessing memory, remembering. Cues or prompts for these strategies can be reviewed and/or displayed to revive/access prior learning.

1. Students (individually; in small groups; as a whole class) remember and list causes of the American Civil War. (Students share list items; a class list of causes is displayed.)
2. Referring to the class textbook, students record data and other information about each of the causes on the class list. (Each small group can be assigned to record about one cause.)
3. Students access well-respected resources (e.g., National Park Service = https://www.nps.gov; Smithsonian Institution = https://www.si.edu) to gather additional information and data related to the causes of the Civil War shared in the class textbook.
4. Each student or each small group chart what these resources say:

Cause   Textbook Information   Other resource information

1. A class discussion explores questions like these:
   a. How are the information and data the same in the text and other resources?
   b. How are the information and data different?
   c. Why are there differences?

    d. Predict how a person might understand the causes of the Civil War by reading only one of these.

    e. What should the textbook company be told about our discussion to improve future editions of our textbook?

2. ASSESSMENT

    a. Depending on the ideas shared in class about question 5e, students draft letters that can be sent to the publishers of the text. (A composite letter could be created or a set of three letters could be "nominated" by the class as a whole.)

    b. If no significant information needs to be sent to the publishing company, assessment of this lesson can occur based on lesson expectations, application of the habit of mind, and extent of student learning.

- *Subject area content:* Applying the strategies learned earlier, students—in small groups, individually, as an entire class—remember and list causes of the Civil War. (Depending on the learning needs of students revealed at this point in the lesson, a teacher can use Gestalt of Choice to adjust the lesson by engaging all students to create a comprehensive class list of causes.)
- *Prior learning:* After finishing a list of causes, students paraphrase (i.e., verbally, or in writing) what the textbook used regularly in class relates about each cause. (Textbook information may include data, rationales, or other details relevant to each cause.)
- *Active learning:* Students—individually or in small groups—use what has been paraphrased from the textbook to analyze other resources about the causes of the Civil War. (As illustrated in Textbox 12.1, resources from the National Park Service and the Smithsonian Institution provide information about the causes of the Civil War.)
- *Fluid intelligence:* Students identify and paraphrase similarities and differences (*compare and contrast*) the information provided by each resource with the information shared by the textbook. After identifying how each resource describes each cause of the Civil War, students discuss the questions shown in Textbox 12.1.
- *Analyze/Create:* Using the ideas expressed in response to these questions, students compose a written evaluation about the textbook coverage of the causes of the Civil War. The evaluation can suggest improvements, questions, and/or appreciation about the coverage of the causes of the Civil War. Finished drafts of this evaluation can be sent to the textbook publisher.

DYNAMIC INSTRUCTION AND INTELLIGENCE

A trio of reflections suggest the student-centric value of *leading-out* intelligence during dynamic instruction:

1. Intelligence is expressed in countless ways. Public educators have a duty to engage all students with *how to think* so that intelligence is the capacity of every student for successful adulthood and citizenship. The complexity inherent in engaging multiple student-intelligences is addressed when an educator uses Gestalt of Choice to ensure that dynamic instruction is responsive to the interrelations in the ecologies of learning represented by the students in class.
2. In the intersection of dynamic instruction and the universe of discourse, public educators interact with Gestalt of Choice to engage all students and lead-out *how to think* on behalf of the common good. This interaction incorporates attention to and behaviors related to the values of the moral obligation of public education.
3. Knowledge about the developmental stages of intelligence and brain function, are especially helpful to public educators (Bloom, 1956, Wolfe, 2001, Krathwohl, 2002). Knowledge about intelligence and brain function evolves. Gestalt of Choice, thus, must be flexible and modified over time alongside research. A functionally public education evolves and public educators persistently improve the ideas in the universe of discourse, the practices and priorities of Gestalt of Choice, and the strategic reciprocities that guide dynamic instruction.

Intelligence and Instruction: Student-Centric Insights

When dynamic instruction introduces, expands, or improves *how to think,* students encounter learning experiences that engage their capacities for meaning-making. "Meaning-making is 'a developmental measure of how individuals organize their experience, which evolves over time' (Ignelzi, 2000, p. 10)" (Swensson, Ellis, and Shaffer, 2019a, 26).

Dynamic instruction is professional behavior designed to account for this development by pursuing "intelligence as the global or composite capacity of an individual to act purposefully, to think rationally, and to deal effectively with the surroundings or situation" (Labby, Lunenburg, and Slate, 2012, 3).

To incorporate the developmental nature of meaning-making through dynamic instruction, educators can assess student expressions of crystallized and/or fluid intelligence. As shown in Figure 12.1, these two generalizations about intelligence allow educators to assess student thinking represented in developmental stages (e.g., *remember, understand, apply,* and *analyze, evaluate, create*).

Student-centric insights about intelligence and instruction begin with the well-researched notion that intelligence evolves and that "stages" provide mile-markers along a student's journey to develop *how to think.* Developmental stages act as cues for applying Gestalt of Choice and for incorporating constructs within the universe of discourse. Using Gestalt of Choice, educators can access relevant cues to orient dynamic instruction and formative assessment.

Dynamic instruction guided by Gestalt of Choice (e.g., selection of an interrelationship between students' developmental stages of intelligence and the lesson content accessed via the universe of discourse) puts public educators in position to lead-out *how to think* in the classroom.

Bloom (1956), Kohlberg and Hersh (1977), Krathwohl (2002), and Piaget (1952) are among the scholars whose work on developmental stages of intelligence provide useful resources for the universe of discourse crafted by public educators.

Emotional Intelligence and Instruction

Every public educator knows that the primary purpose of US public education cannot ignore the role of emotional intelligence in every classroom.

"Salovey and Mayer (1990) coined the term 'emotional intelligence' and defined it as 'the ability to monitor one's own and others' feelings, to discriminate among them, and to use this information to guide one's thinking and actions' (p. 189)" (Labby, Lunenburg, and Slate, 2012, 3).

In every classroom, every day, emotions and human physiology get tangled. The role of emotional intelligence in the realm of teaching and learning exemplifies how Gestalt of Choice is a whole that is more than the sum of its parts. Dynamic instruction must account for this potential cognitive and behavioral traffic jam.

A learning traffic jam is can occur in the ecology of any classroom because "the open-loop design of the limbic system means that other people can change our very physiology—and so our emotions" (Goleman, Boyatzis, and McKee, 2004, 7). Human beings—students and educators—are susceptible to the external influence of others to the point that physical reactions and related behaviors develop.

The dependence of the limbic system on external sources for its management explains why a student who is bullied often exhibits physiological symptoms like crying, expressing anger, or lashing out.

"An open-loop system depends largely on external sources to manage itself" (Goleman, Boyatzis, and McKee, 2004, 6). Because educators also are subject to emotions "managed" by external sources (aka, other people), emotional intelligence must be called upon during dynamic instruction to understand and respond to behaviors sparked by anger, embarrassment, discrimination, humiliation, or fatigue.

When behaviors, communications, experiences, and/or marginalization visited upon students by others spark physical reactions, educators see emotional intelligence "in operation" and have a chance to access their own emotional intelligence to parlay student responses into learnable moments.

The nexus between emotion and physical reactions can be, as public educators know, a significant obstacle to student learning. The importance of the values of the moral obligation of public education reveals the "more than the sum of its parts" interrelationships crafted by educators. Working as "external sources" that positively orient a student's emotional intelligence, the values of moral obligation engaged via the moral agency of a public educator can restore a student's readiness for and engagement with learning.

OBSTACLE-ILLUSIONS: DISTORTIONS IN THE MARKETPLACE

Standardization, discussed earlier, offers attenuated teaching strategies (e.g., standardized testing, teacher-proof instructional materials, virtual learning) for the mishmash of ideologically aligned learning advertised to parents/caregivers and associated with the tenets of free market theory.

Several of these *obstacle-illusions* distort the day-to-day shortcomings of standardization and prevent parents/caregivers from perceiving the limitations imposed by free market theory.

A First Illusion: Education for All

Free market schooling is cloaked in the multilayered illusion that choice education is "(a) more effective and (b) less costly, while (c) serving the same children as regular district schools" (Baker, Libby, and Wiley, 2012, 2).

This illusion implies that marketplace schools are the "more effective" home of learning for all students when compared to traditional public education. This illusion obscures enrollment restrictions and outright discriminatory practices that prohibit innumerable students from enrollment, much less learning, in free market schools.

In addition, data about privatization education reveals high student dropout and failure-to-attend rates (Swensson, Ellis, and Shaffer, 2019a). The illusion of "education for all" is revealed when enrollment numbers used to advertise educational value and the popularity of privatization mechanisms evaporate, and hide not only attenuated attendance but, in some cases, leave fraud as residue.

A Second Illusion: Amorality Is a Moral Obligation

The educational marketplace, as has been discussed, promotes a dog-eat-dog competition among schools and students. Validated as merely the cost of doing business, this level of amorality in the marketplace (Lubienski, 2013) becomes its oxymoronic expression of moral obligation.

Just like default choice, amorality is a simple justification of "winners" and "losers." Amorality separates *the public* from the values of moral obligation at the foundation of US democracy.

The obligation of the marketplace to amorality generates illusions that obstruct student-centric principles:

- Free market theory supposes that a student's lack of academic success is a matter of individual failings.
- Learning devolves into a one-on-one encounter between students and predigested instruction.
- To insulate themselves against "losers," and to fulfill the obligations of theory, free market schools embrace amorality by setting up shop near neighborhoods where predetermined enrollees (e.g., economic, racial, ethnic cohorts) and their families live (Swensson, Ellis, and Shaffer, 2019b).
- Amorality is carte blanche for privatization schools to charge extra fees and operate in locations where state or local statutes turn a blind eye to segregation (Swensson and Shaffer, 2020).

The illusions of schooling for all and amorality as moral obligation ensure that standardized instruction predominates in the marketplace. The validation that proponents and enrollees feel from buying illusions speaks to the power of "freedom" generated by amorality.

INSTRUCTION AND THE COMMON GOOD

The moral obligation of US public education is a keystone of citizenship in democracy. The values of this obligation engage students with the common good.

These values include "'overarching principles [that] have been agreed on in our society and within the teaching profession—principles dealing with honesty, fairness, protection of the weak, and respect for all people' (Clark, 1990, p. 252)" (Campbell, 2008, 602).

Moral Obligation Abandoned

Moral obligation is abandoned and the common good is forsaken when US education reflects beliefs such as those shared by Eng (2013), who writes that "inequality in the outcomes of schooling is a function of the natural inequality of talent among people (Ornstein, 1977), due to the different mental patterns and thinking processes that are shaped by both genetics and environmental forces" (280).

Eng's pernicious assertion is a racist falsehood (Hampton, 2016; Worrell, 2013). Eng's point of view and others like it marginalize large numbers of students. Uncritical habits of mind like this denigrate the "I identify as . . ." statements of US students (Swensson, Ellis, and Shaffer, 2019b) and, as such, bolster the amorality aligned with the tenets of free market theory.

Free market schooling is a license to deny equity, achievement, respect, and social justice. In effect, the abandonment of governmental oversight, the dedication to singularity, and the prevalence of disdain for the "other" have the potential to invite policies and behaviors that share:

- *Deficit-thinking*: "When any adult assumes, without justification of any kind, that cohorts of students cannot be successful, teaching and other interactions demonstrate deficit-thinking" (Swensson and Shaffer, 2020, 72). Deficit-thinking enshrines stereotypes and prejudice in adult behaviors that deny student capacities for learning and school success (Furman, 2012). Discredited assumptions about the genetic predisposition of various racial, religious, or ethnic groups to lack the capacity for higher order thinking sustain bigoted behaviors that express deficit-thinking.
- *Racial opportunity cost*: Racial opportunity cost is paid by students of color when "at issue is not whether a student is actually smart or academically capable, but rather whether their presentation of *smart* and *capable* is judged to be correct" (emphasis original) (Chambers, Huggins, Locke, and Fowler, 2014, 467). Ending payment of racial opportunity cost means ending reliance on presentation as if it defines intelligence or meaning-making. Engaging all students with habits of mind, educators accelerate the capacity for *how to think* which facilitates assessment of thinking not presentation.

- *Stereotype threat*: When students "believe that their performance is being judged by others who have [a] stereotype in mind" (Worrell, 2014, 339), stereotype threat occurs. The developmentally appropriate universal audience that early adolescents and young people envision heightens awareness about and the negative effect of perceived stereo-typic judgment. Paying the toll of racism, students of color face stereo-typic accountability that dismantles their cognitive expressions with a jackhammer of denial.
- *Marginalization*: "Marginalization is the emotional, behavioral, and/or cognitive rendering 'other' human beings peripheral" (Swensson and Shaffer, 2020, 72). Deficit thinking, racial opportunity cost, and stereo-type threat are the malign tools of marginalization. Behaviors, communications, and nonverbal indicators that employ these tools disconnect adults from moral obligation and discard the values of moral obligation that all students deserve.

These impediments establish environments in which students and learning are constrained. Under the influence of uncritical habits of mind, students are susceptible to entanglements between emotional intelligence and physiological reactions.

The means employed to construct the educational marketplace leave vast swathes of marketplace schooling disconnected from the values of moral obligation. Abandoning the values of moral obligation and subverting the meaning-making necessary to reflect and act upon these values, free market schooling desiccates the capacities of students to enact the common good.

The Impact of Dynamic Instruction

"Dynamic instruction entails 'the cyclical relation between emotional and instructional supports' (Curby, Rimm-Kaufman, and Abry, 2013, p. 566) that exemplify the professional practices undertaken in the intersection between *how to think* and moral obligation" (Swensson and Shaffer, 2020, 21).

Instead of linear expectations about inputs and outputs posing as education, dynamic instruction embraces expectations for student engagement (cognitive, emotional, and behavioral) with what scholars have termed *evolutionary learning* (Kurth-Schai, 2014, 434).

Dynamic instruction is the professional engagement of public educators with the capacities that allow student meaning-making to flourish. Dynamic instruction puts traditional public educators in position to narrate a student-centric purpose for the history of the future of US education.

Chapter 13

A Future for Learning

EMAIL
To: Traditional Public Educators
Fr: Your Future Colleagues
Re: One Narrative Is the Future for All Students

The battle to write the narrative for the history of the future for traditional public education, cannot be separated from learning. Traditional public educators, all of us, pursue our student-centric purpose while being battered by marketeers and free market tenets divorced from *how to think* in pursuit of the common good.

Nevertheless, we persevere.

In large measure, traditional public educators persevere because the professional resources and capabilities used in public school classrooms constitute service on behalf of something greater than self.

Public educators accept responsibility, are accountable for, and are obliged to fulfill a purpose beyond mere self-aggrandizement.

Yet, choice to take the journey of traditional public education is subject to multiple impediments. The road along which public educators now travel is subject to the landslides of history, the potholes of ideology, and the detours imposed by insufficiency.

The final chapter in this discussion confirms, despite this difficult journey, that traditional public educators are in position to overcome the factors and forces that attempt to write an adult-centric narrative for the history of the future of America's schooling.

Illuminated throughout this book, choice about learning depends on contemporary public educators' understanding that they are writing the history of the future of traditional public education necessary and sufficient to fulfill the balance between individual goals and the principles of US democracy.

Of utmost importance to all US students—the adults, voters, economic engines, creative beacons, and thinkers of the future—is that traditional public educators assert their professional capabilities and dynamic resources to resolve the struggle over choice about learning.

WHICH CHOICE, WHICH NARRATIVE, WHICH FUTURE?

Choices, narratives, and futures are at stake in the struggle between proponents of the two major perspectives about US education. When all is said and done, this struggle is a contest to determine what's socially valuable in US democracy.

One perspective entails a choice to prepare all students with learning necessary and sufficient to encounter personal success and citizenship amid the "unfixed" world, unknowns, ambiguities, and adaptive challenges in the future.

For advocates of traditional public education, the reciprocal relationship between history and the future is the journey during which milestones along the way identify progress toward what's natural to education including *how to think,* the common good, and the values of the moral obligation of public education.

The other perspective is a choice of the destination where preselected cohorts of students are prepared to follow the tenets of free market theory.

For proponents of privatization education, there is little distance between history and the future. Bound together by the tenets of free market theory and adult-centric intentions, the relationship between history and a future determined by educational choice creates an efficient, cheap, and uncomplicated marketplace. Singularity, disdain, and public dissonance become things natural to education.

Decisions about how students ought to engage with learning and decisions about the purpose of US education are underway. Although numerous players exert influence over choice for the narrative of the future, traditional public educators have the resources and capacities required to write the final draft.

This is not to say, though, that a student-centric narrative for learning in traditional public education is guaranteed for the future.

Back to the Past: On the Way to the Destination

If the future is a narrative inspired by interpretations of the past that align with and justify contemporary individual ideology, then marketplace schooling is a destination where the past and the future are one in the same.

Adult-centric intentions that constitute this destination limit and restrict participation in learning. Such a future evokes commentary from the 1800's when "the *Chicago Tribune* editorialized against the preposterous idea of pre-paring 'the children of working men' for college, and called summer school courses for poor students 'alluring luxuries'" (Goldstein, 2015, 68).

The struggle over choice about educational choice is a battle to ensure that learning is subservient to free market theory. Proponents of marketplace education compete with America's traditional public education as a foe to be vanquished.

When Going Backward Is Identified as Going Forward

All the previous chapters in this book hint at the fundamental flaw of priva-tization education: privatization education and its proponents point forward and move backward. Claiming one thing but delivering another, marketplace schooling is its own contradiction of its supposed educational choices:

- Free market infatuation with standardized testing constitutes learning as a falsehood. Instead of engaging students to empower their practical, creative, and analytical contributions to a future economy, privatization handcuffs learning to familiar patterns. An ironclad allegiance to free market theory yields schooling incapable of moving forward.
- The point-forward-go-backward results of increasing numbers of char-ter schools and a comprehensive voucher program for private school students is illustrated by Indiana's experience. "From 2000 to 2020, traditional public school enrollment actually rose by more than 62,000 kids. *After choice came, and schools began competing for students, the winners were local public schools*" (Hicks, 2022).
- Privatization education proponents claim an abiding interest in a robust economy and highly qualified employees. This claim, however, is nothing less than the backward motion of privatization: students are distanced from learning, standardized testing prioritizes lower-order cognition, and free market strategies drain funding from schools serving 90 percent of America's students. Backing up yields an insufficient num-ber of well-prepared employees whose academic insufficiencies develop from an underfunded traditional public education system (Briggs, 2022).
- Insufficient funding for traditional public education and increasing support for privatization yields a state unable to educate its students to participate in their own and the state's economic success. In Indiana, "inflation-adjusted spending per K-12 student was 17% lower in 2020 than it was in 2010" (Briggs, 2022, 24A).
- A classic catch-22 emerges from the backward and downward spiral inspired by the pursuit of free market education. "Indiana is one of the

worst states in the nation for educational attainment, so companies that do business here tailor their operations to the workforce they have" (Briggs, 2022, 24A). Reliance on marketplace education portends the demise of its supposed advantages.

IN THE LONG RUN, DEFAULT
CHOICE IS ITS OWN FAULT

Default choice, the lead-in to privatization education, receives a great deal of attention in the twenty-first century. Ideologues, citizens, media representatives, foundations, politicians, and some educators focus on the ease, the self-aggrandizement, and the ROI that result from default choice.

But, all the hubbub, all the claims, all the statutes, all the consumer relations, all the promises and guarantees are nothing more substantial than fog. Privatization education depends on this fog of certainty to cover up the devastation intended in a marketplace:

1. *Marketplace education specializes in indoctrination.* Free market theory, intentions that include singularity and competition, separation and division of students, attenuation of learning from sufficient funding—all represent the principles of the marketplace that students are expected to learn as the ROI derived from what-to-think.

2. *Marketplace education recycles and sustains* poverty, racism, and discrimination. Free market schooling perpetuates the life costs paid by too many US students. Restricting enrollment and fostering marginalization, marketeers are clear about who deserves to learn and who does not. "In most states, the resources expended by the highest-poverty districts are well below what would be required for these students to perform at average levels, and in some states, actual spending is but a small fraction of the estimated requirement" (Baker, DiCarlo, and Weber, 2019, 13). Then, adding insult to injury, proponents of privatization blame those who are turned away when the insufficiencies forced on public schools prevent higher-level learning and an effective "fit" with the economic needs of the nation.

3. *Marketplace education is designed to assail* and dismantle its competition, traditional public education. Creating what amounts to a self-fulfilling prophecy, advocates of the educational marketplace attack traditional public education with statutes, educational gerrymandering, and ideological disdain. Proponents of marketplace education create, reinforce, and perpetuate the deficiencies that become the inadequacies

for which traditional public education is criticized from a free market perspective.

4. *Marketplace education is permanent economic denial.* Despite the emphasis of free market theory on profit and "winning," economic denial arises from marketplace education when limits are placed on who learns and what is learned. The restrictions built into free market education and the assault by marketeers on the supposed burdens of traditional public education detain the potential of the nation's students and, thus, the nation's economy. The free market intention "that students are in school primarily to acquire marketable skills to be cashed in for employment" (Strike, 2008, 121) is self-regulating in the sense that only enrollees in privatization education are "the fittest" for economic success. "Others" are relegated permanently to insufficiently funded traditional public education where marketable skills are limited to employment in cost-efficient low-wage jobs.

Default choice leads to numerous dead ends. Not only is learning immobilized under the auspices of free market schooling, but the future stagnates because it builds on the disconnections and separations of ROI that dictate an incomplete, limited, history for the future of personal, economic, and civic success in the future.

Default choice is a commitment to an ideology for education whose promises are marketplace platitudes.

Default choice is the momentum established by adult-centric intentions to contradict the existence of traditional public education: "the distinct organizational orientation toward profit maximization often becomes incompatible with collective purposes required in publicly offered products and services" (Lee, 2018, 5).

WRENCHES IN THE WORKS OF THE CLOSED LOOP SYSTEM

At the end of the day, three wrenches are embedded in the closed loop system of marketplace schooling. The intentions of this destination are disrupted because marketeers fail to acknowledge that:

1. Improved learning seems to be immune to schooling based on adult-centric intentions. In response to this frustration, marketplace education adherents have abandoned claims of academic superiority for privatization education. Paradoxically, marketeers label neglect of student achievement as a victory for the priorities of free market ideology

(Strauss, 2016). Choice about educational choice yields schooling dedicated to ideological principles, not student learning.

2. Although insufficient funding for traditional public education is responsible for downsizing, and although insufficiencies in funding are tied to
   mechanisms and gerrymandering that finance free market education,
   proponents of privatization education appear to be dissatisfied with the
   turbulence created by these circumstances and by the lackluster revenue
   supplied to marketplace schools. To remedy these frustrations, free market advocates double down on *accountability to* free market theory with
   a surprising solution.

   Marketeers look forward to the future when efficient, low-cost,
   and competitive schooling fostered by default choice will transform
   America's schools to the point that privatization education "will ultimately be funded by taxpayers" (Rogers, 2015, 748). Investment in
   marketplace education via taxation, it turns out, is acceptable so long as
   government-generated funding supports ideological imperatives.

3. "The Other," for adherents of free market schooling is a foe. Fending off
   others who are unworthy of "winning" in the marketplace is a feature
   of adult-centric intentions. To this end, free market proponents unleash
   singularity, public dissonance, fiscal insufficiency, discrimination, and
   disdain to dismantle traditional public education and prevent unwel-
   come "consumers" from marketplace participation. Adult-centric intentions ensure that significantly increased resources required for students
   in poverty are unavailable (Black, 2019, 1402).

ON BEHALF OF ALL US STUDENTS

Au (2010) highlights the original Greek root of idiocy, *idios, which means
"private, self-centered, selfish, and separate"* (8).

A destination that guarantees a self-centered US education overrun with
singularity, profit, "losers," and dog-eat-dog competition is pure *idios*. The
idiocy of adult-centric intentions that constitute marketplace education is prioritized at the expense of *how to think* on behalf of the common good.

To Win the Match: Hit the Ball Back Over the Net

As daunting as the intentions and purpose of free market education appears,
traditional public educators are two "serves" away from a future of learning
that all students deserve. The first serve is an "ace" powered by research
about funding and learning. The second serve delivers the conclusion for this
titanic struggle: student-centric resources and professional capabilities.

First Serve: Learning Deserves Sufficient Funding

The inadequacies and platitudes of free market education cannot obscure the faults and failures embedded in a narrative where ideology supplants traditional US public education.

Accessing research, traditional public educators "return serve" to marketeers. The extent of the enduring *failure of less* imposed on students and society by marketplace proponents is confirmed when:

- Jackson, Johnson, and Persico (2016) found "that a 25% increase in per pupil spending throughout the school-age years could eliminate the attainment gaps between children from low-income and nonpoor families" (214).
- Weathers and Sosina (2019) point out that "achievement outcomes for low-income students were highest in states that invested more in education" (6).
- Connecticut took aim at disparities among school districts through a focus on low-wealth districts and the need for resources to improve instruction in those localities. By 1986, NAEP results for fourth graders in both reading and math put Connecticut first in the nation. Reading and writing proficiency for 8th graders, at the same time, rose to first in the nation while Connecticut's students were out-performed in science in the world only by Singapore (Darling-Hammond, 2019).
- Funding directed at the most important task of education (e.g., dynamic instruction and the original power of education) yields significant academic success for students (Baker, 2016; Jackson, Johnson, and Persico, 2016).
- "Research-proven supports and interventions include high-quality pre-school, extended learning time, smaller class sizes, in- and out-of-class tutoring, sufficient guidance counselors and nurses, and access to social and mental health services" (Farrie, Kim, and Sciarra, 2019, 12).
- "The states ranked highest on *Education Week's* 2017 Quality Counts K-12 achievement index have per-pupil spending well above the national average of $11,454" (Partelow, Shapiro, McDaniels, and Brown, 2018, "Money Matters in Education," para. 5).
- "For low-income children, a 10% increase in per pupil spending each year for all 12 years of public school is associated with 0.46 additional years of completed education, 9.6% higher earnings, and a 6.1 percentage point reduction in the annual incidence of adult poverty" (Jackson, Johnson, and Persico, 2016, 160).

Second Serve: The Core Competencies of Traditional Public Educators

Core competencies are the professional capabilities of traditional public educators that deliver RTS in the ecology of classrooms: learning derived from the universe of discourse, the elements in an educator's Gestalt of Choice, and the original power of education expressed in dynamic instruction.

Core competencies are the capacity of traditional public educators to write a student-centric narrative for the history of the future of traditional US public education.

Core competencies engage with and improve the attributes of intelligence—analytic, creative, and practical—that students derive from learning *how to think*. Reflection and action associated with learning at this level puts students in position to make sense out of, and contribute to, their lives. Meaning-making also engages all students with the ongoing construction of balance for citizenship in US democracy.

Core competencies constitute what's natural to education as an evolving journey of meaning-making. These professional choices connect *how to think* and the values of the moral obligation of public education on behalf of growing, expanding, and challenging student intelligences.

Some core competencies play a role in Gestalt of Choice of all public educators. Other core competencies will depend on the grade level, subject area, and prior learning of students. Still additional core competencies will emerge as student learning expands into new knowledge realms or as student learning reveals the need to re-teach or re-examine prior learning. Core competencies improve and expand further as educators utilize evolving research.

Under these circumstances, the value of Gestalt of Choice becomes apparent. This array of knowledge, skills, research, and prior experience that constitutes a public educator's professional judgment—composed from four-year university training, ongoing teaching experience, and persistent development of student-centric teaching strategies—is the essential ingredient in the nexus between the universe of discourse and dynamic instruction.

Resources necessary and sufficient for writing a student-centric narrative are readily available to all traditional public educators. Access to and the sustained value of these resources are enhanced when:

- *Purpose is shared.* Public educators are exceptional communicators. To break the grip of fear that instills disdain, public educators must extend their communications to the school community. "Tell your story" means explaining early and often, during every school year, the purpose for engaging all students with *how to think* in pursuit of the common good (Swensson, Ellis, and Shaffer, 2019a).

- *Turbulence is defused.* Although turbulence generated by disdain is difficult to defuse, the turbulence generated among parents/caregivers can be assuaged. Talking with parents/caregivers one-on-one about what happens in class during teaching and learning instills trust where turbulence is invoked falsely. Because traditional public educators focus on students, these conversations illustrate learning and progress in the lives of students that prepare them to flourish.
- *Available resources are prioritized.* Organizational decline and reduced resources go hand in hand. Insufficient fiscal resources exacerbate disdain for traditional public education. But, once public educators focus on available resources—core competencies, dynamic instruction, the values of moral obligation, the original power of education—an ecology of learning exists. As a result, every classroom can be an ecology where the promise in every student is maximized and the promises in the principles of democracy are sustained.

THE NARRATIVE OF CORE COMPETENCIES

The narrative of core competencies is written in the "teacher mediated process that assists students in effectively gaining the knowledge skills, capabilities and moral dispositions that are of value in expanding their freedoms" (Reimers, 2006, 281).

Freedoms expand when the original power of education and the exchange of intelligences in a public school classroom build the agency required for students to balance individual rights with the moral obligations of citizenship in US democracy.

The value of Gestalt of Choice lies in its power to access, convey, demonstrate, share, and assess the core competencies within the ecology of any classroom to expand freedoms in this way.

Research points to the overwhelming impact of in-person dynamic instruction on student learning. "Instruction trumps programs, student grouping patterns, choice arrangements, and all other school factors (Supovitz and Turner, 2000; Wahlstrom and Louis, 2008)" (Murphy et al., 2016, 456). The core competencies of traditional public educators engage all learners with student-centric goals including:

- "The purpose of education is to develop not only knowledge and skills, but the ability to *use* one's knowledge and skills effectively" (emphasis added) (Sternberg, Reznitskaya, and Jarvin, 2007, 144).

- Taking its cue from these intimations of the primary purpose for traditional US public education, learning is defined as "the student's power of cognitive ownership" (Swensson and Shaffer, 2020, 68).
- "A good public school prepares students for "the 'unfixed' social world for which young people will be learning" (McWilliam, 2008, 264).
- The role of public education incorporates skills and knowledge that foster and grow citizenship engagement for all students (Gutmann and Ben-Porah, 2015) because democracy is the central feature of America's unfixed social world.
- Traditional US public educators accept the obligation to "prepare all students to recognize and accept the basic equality among all persons, even as the achievement of this imperative is always a work in progress" (Reimers, 2006, 282).
- The application of core competencies daily by traditional public educators demonstrates why "a number of studies have found that greater spending on instruction, especially the quality of teachers, tends to provide stronger leverage on student achievement than many other uses of funds" (Darling-Hammond, 2019, 7).
- Virtue is a foundation from which educators attend to the relationship between the original power of education and US democracy. The purpose of this relationship is to "develop in young people both the knowledge and skills that individuals need to live free lives and the shared values . . . that citizens need to support the institutions that enable them to live freely" (Gutmann and Ben-Porah, 2015, 1).

The Consequences of Choice about Learning

The purpose of traditional public education is to provide students with capabilities for a fruitful life as an individual and as a citizen. Innumerable consequences of this purpose speak to the social value of an RTS (return to students) narrative. The consequences of this narrative include:

- All students learning beyond capacities developed before formal learning experiences. This means that thinking, "an automatic cognitive response to daily living based on individual perceptions of ideas, interactions, and situations that arise" (Richart and Perkins, 2005), is a resource nurtured and expanded in the ecology of public school classrooms for all students.
- Instruction designed to be accountable *for* student engagement with higher-order thinking and dispositions. *Accountability for* all students entails the reflexivity of the original power of education that "cultivate[s] a sense of empathy for others, patience, tolerance

self-discipline, courage, personal responsibility, mutual respect, and honesty" (Campbell, 2008, 608).

- Public reciprocity, which entails "'seeing the world from several different points of view, connecting ideas and/or finding patterns among ideas, imagining alternatives and possibilities, and determining the relevance of ideas, data, and points of view' (Schmoker (2006) p. 58)" (Swensson, Ellis, and Shaffer, 2019a, 21–22).
- Continuous interplay between reflection and action to access virtue. In an open loop system, public educators access excellence that encompasses both competency and ethics when every day to day choice accepts the responsibility "to serve the 'best interests of the student'" (Stefkovich and Begley, 2007, 212).

WHO WILL WRITE THE HISTORY OF THE FUTURE OF US PUBLIC EDUCATION?

Although narrating the history of the future of US public education is an extraordinarily complex undertaking, traditional public educators possess the wherewithal to overcome obstacles and compose a narrative for US education that accommodates all students and their futures.

Traditional public educators have the core competencies capable of accessing and implementing resources designed to fulfill student-centric intentions. Gestalt of Choice and dynamic instruction are applicable in any ecology of learning in any classroom.

Writing the history of the future of traditional US public education is in the hands of "successful teachers [who] are not simply charismatic, persuasive and expert presenters; rather, they create powerful cognitive and social tasks to their students and teach the students how to make productive use of them" (Hopkins, 2003, 61).

It turns out that traditional public education continues to offer the choice about learning with the greatest impact on all students and, thus, on the future of US democracy. The narrative about the history of the future of traditional US public education with the greatest social value is a purpose greater than self.

Traditional public educators make this student-centric choice every day. Thus, when traditional public educators say *the future is now* they accept responsibility for choice about learning and ensure that the futures of all students and the success of US democracy are the function, the purpose, of traditional US education.

Epilogue

Our Common Fate Together

Educators in traditional US public schools, as this book indicates, share common intentions, student-centric instruction, and a purpose dedicated to *how to think* on behalf of the common good. This is the common fate together composed by traditional public educators and sought on behalf of all students and US democracy.

But, traditional public educators do not share a statement that conveys this student-centric resolution and purpose held in common. To that end, public educators can summarize what's socially valuable about a future of learning in student-centric classrooms throughout traditional public education in a public educator's oath:

THE PUBLIC EDUCATOR'S OATH

I am a public school teacher. I accept responsibility for engaging all my students with learning. I am accountable for things greater than myself including citizenship education for social justice in US democracy. I am obligated to act with personal and professional integrity at all times. I focus my professional practices on dynamic instruction and the common good. I am dedicated to effective teamwork with colleagues, strong communication with parents/caregivers, and respectful engagement with our school community.

Adopting this statement, or one like it, makes explicit the day-to-day and future commitment of traditional public educators to a student-centric purpose.

A RECKONING WITH LEARNING

A reckoning with learning is the heart of the Public Educator's Oath. The time has come for the public work (Boyte, 2011) of traditional public educators to employ an oath to confirm and make explicit the student-centric purpose of US education. Knight Abowitz (2018) summarizes public work as "'self-organized efforts by a mix of people who solve common problems and create things, material or symbolic, of lasting civic value (p. 632–633)'" (8).

All students deserve formal learning experiences crafted via Gestalt of Choice to acquire cognitive behaviors necessary and sufficient to confront a future laden with adaptive challenges which "are problems for which there is not an existing or predefined solution" (Douglass, 2018, p. 388). The civic value of traditional public education is found in citizenship capable of ethical responses to adaptive challenges.

As Knight Abowitz and Stitzlein (2018) observe, public schools "can create the conditions for an educated citizenry with the knowledge and capacity for working with diverse others in negotiating our common fate together" (p. 37). A coalition of current and future public educators, via Gestalt of Choice and the original power of education, exists to choose the narrative of *how to think* on behalf of the common good.

A reckoning with the struggle over the purpose for America's education is past due. The time has come for traditional public educators to bypass the marketplace and assert the purpose and professional expertise that prioritizes student-centric learning in traditional US public education. Bright futures for all US students and for the nation's democracy require nothing less.

References

Abdulkadiroglu, A., P. A. Pathak, and C. R. Walters (2015, December). School Vouchers and Student Achievement: Evidence from the Louisiana Scholarship Program. *Working Paper 21839.* Cambridge, MA: National Bureau of Economic Research. Retrieved from http://www.nber.org/papers/w21839.

AFT (American Federation of Teachers). (2018). *A Decade of Neglect: Public Education Funding in the Aftermath of the Great Recession.* Washington, DC: American Federation of Teachers.

Anderson, G. L., and L M. Donchik (2016). Privatizing Schooling and Policy Making: The American Legislative Exchange Council and New Political and Discursive Strategies of Education Governance. *Educational Policy, (30)*2, 322–64. doi:10.1177/0895904814528794.

Au, W. (2010). The Idiocy of Policy: The Anti-Democratic Curriculum of High-Stakes Testing. *Critical Education (1)*1, 1–15. Retrieved from https://doi.org/10.14288/ce.v1i1.182239.

Baker, B. D., D. Farrie, and D. G. Sciarra (2016). *Mind the Gap: 20 Years of Progress and Retrenchment in School Funding and Achievement Gaps.* (Policy Information Report and ETS Research Report Series No. RR-16–15). Princeton, NJ: Education Testing Service. doi:10.1002/ets2.12098.

Baker, B. D., M. DiCarlo, and M. Weber, M. (2019). The Adequacy and Fairness of State School Finance Systems. Findings from the School Finance Indicators Database, School Year 2015–2016. Washington, DC: Albert Shanker Institute. Retrieved from www.schoolfinancedata.org.

Baker, B. D., K. Libby, and K. Wiley (2012). *Spending by the Major Charter Management Organizations: Comparing Charter School and Local Public District Financial Resources in New York, Ohio, and Texas.* Boulder, CO: National Education Policy Center. Retrieved from http://nepc.colorado.edu/publication/spending-major-charter.

Baker, B. D., and G. Miron (2015, December). *The Business of Charter Schooling: Understanding the Policies that Charter Operators Use for Financial Benefit.* Boulder, CO: National Education Policy Center. Retrieved from http://nepc.colorado.edu/publiatin/charter-revenue.

Banks, J. (1973). *Teaching Strategies for the Social Studies: Inquiry, Valuing, and Decision-making.* Reading, MA: Addison-Wesley Publishing Company.

Barnum, M. (2018a). Why One Harvard Professor Calls American School's Focus on Testing a "Charade." *Chalkbeat.* January 19, 2018. Retrieved from https://www .chalkbeat.org/posts/us/2018/01/19/why-one-harvard-professor.

Barnum, M. (2018b). Virtual Schools, Open Records, and Claims about Research—Highlights from Congress's Look at Charter Schools. *Chalkbeat.* June 13, 2018. Retrieved from http://www.chalkbeat.com/posts/us/2018/06/13/virtual-schools -open.

Barrow, L., and C. E. Rouse (2008). School Vouchers: Recent Findings and Unanswered Questions. *Economic Perspectives (3Q).* Chicago: Federal Reserve Bank of Chicago. Retrieved from http://ssrn.com/abstract=1268316.

Belfield, C., and Levin, H. (2005). Vouchers and Public Policy: When Ideology Trumps Evidence. *American Journal of Education (111)*4, 548–67. doi:10.1086/431183.

Biddle, B. J., and D. C. Berliner (2002, May). Research Synthesis/Unequal Funding in the United States. *Educational Leadership (59)*8, 48–59.

Biesta, G. (2009). Good Education in an Age of Measurement: On the Need to Reconnect with the Question of Purpose in Education. *Educational Assessment, Evaluation and Accountability (21)*1, 33–46. Retrieved from https://doi.org/10 .1007/s11092-008-9064-9.

Black, D. W. (2019, December). Educational Gerrymandering: Money, Motives, and Constitutional Rights. *New York University Law Review (94)*6, 1385–1464.

Bloom, B. (ed.) (1956). *Taxonomy of Educational Objectives: The Classification of Educational Goals.* New York: Longmans Green.

Boesenberg, E. (2003). Privatizing Public Schools: Education in the Marketplace. *Workingplace, 10,* 66–76. Retrieved from https://researchgate.net/315613921 _Privatizing_Public_Schools_Education_in_the_Marketplace.

Bolsen, T. (2013). A Light Bulb Goes On: Norms, Rhetoric, and Actions for the Public Good. *Political Behavior, 35,* 1–20. doi:10.1007/s11109-011-9186-5.

Boser, U., M. Boser, and E. Roth (2018, March 20). *The Highly Negative Impact of Vouchers.* Washington, DC: Center for American Progress.

Bracey, G. W. (2004). *Setting the Record Straight: Responses to Misconceptions About Public Education in the United States.* Portsmouth, NH: Heinemann.

Bracey, G. W. (2009). *Educational Hell: Rhetoric vs. Reality.* Alexandria, VA: Educational Research Service.

Briggs, J. (2022, May 8). Research: Indiana Is a College Degree Desert. *Indianapolis Star, May 8, 2022.* p. 23A, p. 24A.

Brighouse, H., and Mullane, K. (2018). Aims and Purposes of a State Schooling System: The Case of California. (Technical Report). *Policy Analysis for California Education PACE.* Stanford, CA: Stanford University.

Bronfenbrenner, U. (1979). *The Ecology of Human Development: Experiments by Nature and Design.* Cambridge, MA: Harvard University Press.

Brooks, D. (2017, November 16). Our Elites Still Don't Get It. *New York Times.* Retrieved from https://nyti.ms/2jz2uZD.

Brown, E. (2017, April 9). DeVos Praises this Voucher-like Program. Here's What It Means for School Reform. *Washington Post.* Retrieved from https://www .washingtonpost.com/local/education/devos-praises-this-voucher-like-program.

Brown, F. (2002). Privatization of Public Elementary and Secondary Education in the United States of America. *Education and the Law (14)*1–2, 99–114. doi:10.1080/09539960220149218.

Brown, P. C., H. L. Roediger III, and M. A. McDaniel (2014). *Make It Stick: The Science of Successful Learning.* Cambridge, MA: The Belknap Press of Harvard University Press.

Brozo, W. C., and M. L. Simpson (2003). *Readers, Teachers, Learners: Expanding Literacy Across the Content Areas* (4th ed). Upper Saddle River, NJ: Merrill Prentice Hall.

Bruecker, E. (2017). *Assessing the Fiscal Impact of Wisconsin's Statewide Voucher Program.* Boulder, CO: National Education Policy Center.

Cameron, K., and J. McNaughtan (2014). Positive Organizational Change. *Journal of Applied Behavioral Science* 50(4), 445–62.

Campbell, E. (2008). Teaching Ethically as a Moral Condition of Professionalism. In Larry P. Nucci and Darcia Narvaez (eds.), *Handbook of Moral and Character Education,* 601–15. New York: Routledge.

Carey, K., and E. A. Harris (2016, December 12). It Turns Out Spending More Probably Does Improve Education. *New York Times.* Retrieved from http://myti .ms2hfv3YM.

Carlson, D. E., J. M. Cowen, and D. J. Fleming (2013). Third-Party Governance and Performance Measurement: A Case Study of Publicly Funded Private School Vouchers. *Journal of Public Administration Research and Theory (25),* 897–922. doi:10.1093/jopart/mut017.

Chambers, T. V., K. S. Huggins, L. A. Locke, and R. M. Fowler (2014). Between a "ROC" and a School Place: The Role of *Racial Opportunity Cost* in the Educational Experiences of Academically Successful Students of Color. *Educational Studies* 50, 464–97. doi:10.1080/00131946/2014.943891.

Chernow, R. (2004). *Alexander Hamilton.* London: Penguin Press.

Chubb, J. E., and T. M. Moe (1990). *Politics, Markets, and America's Schools.* Washington, DC: The Brookings Institution.

Cierniak, K., R. Billick, and A. M. Ruddy (2015). The Indiana Choice Scholarship Program: Legal Challenges, Program Expansion, and Participation. Bloomington, IN: Center for Evaluation and Education Policy.

Ciulla, J. B., D. Knights, C. Mabey, and L. Tomkins (2018). Philosophical Contributions to Leadership Ethics. *Business Ethics Quarterly (28)*1, 1–14. doi:10.1017/beq.2017.48.

Covey, F. (2020). *The 7 Habits of Highly Effective People.* New York: Simon & Shuster.

Cowen, J. M., D. J. Fleming, J. F. Witte, and P. J. Wolf, P. J. (2012). Going Public: Who Leaves a Large, Longstanding, and Widely Available Urban Voucher Program. *American Educational Research Journal (49)*2, 231–56. doi:10.3102/0002831211424313.

Cubberley, E. P. (1919). *Public Education in the United States: A Study and Interpretation of American Educational History.* Boston: Houghton Mifflin.

Darling, N. (2007). Ecological Systems Theory: The Person in the Center of the Circles. *Research in Human Development (4)*3–4, 203–17.

Darling-Hammond, L. (2019). *Investing for Student Success: Lessons from State School Finance Reforms.* Palo Alto, CA: Learning Policy Institute.

Dawkins-Law, S. E. (2014). Why American Needs a Counterstory to "Choice as the Last Civil Right." *Sanford Journal of Public Policy, (5)*2, 1–20. Retrieved from https://sites.duke.edu/sjpp/files/2014/05/Dawkins-Law.

DeAngelis, C. A., and H. H. Erickson (2018). What Leads to Successful School Choice Programs? A Review of the Theories and Evidence. *Cato Journal (38)*1, 247–60.

DeBray-Pelot, E. H., C. A. Lubienski, and J. T. Scott (2007). The Institutional Landscape of Interest Group Politics and School Choice. *Peabody Journal of Education, (82)*2–3, 204–30. Retrieved from https://gspp.berkeley.edu/assets/uploads/research/pdf/.

Dewey, J. (1916). *Democracy and Education.* Retrieved from www.public-library.uk.

Dewey, J. (1933). *How We Think.* Boston, MA: D. C. Heath.

Douglass, A. (2018). Redefining Leadership: Lessons from an Early Education Leadership Development Initiative. *Early Childhood Education Journal* 46, 387–96. doi:10.1007/s10643-017-0871-9.

Elder, A. (2014, January-March). Do Cyber Charter Schools Help or Hurt the Educational System? *Penn State University Education News.* Retrieved from https://www.ed.psu.edu/educ/news/january-march-2014/cyber-charter.

Eliot, T. S. (1925). *The Hollow Men.* Retrieved from www.icsnc.org.

Elmore, R. F. (2005). Accountable Leadership. *The Educational Forum* 69, 134–42.

Emerson, R. W. (1841). *Self Reliance.* Rockville, MD: Arc Manor Books (2007).

Eng, N. (2013). The Impact of Demographics on 21st Century Education. *Social Science and Public Policy* 50(3), 272–82. doi:10.1007/s12115-013-9655-z.

Farrie, D., R. Kim, and D. Sciarra (2019). *Making the Grade 2019: How Fair Is School Funding in Your State?* (Report). Newark, NJ: Education Law Center.

Fiddiman, B., and J. Yin (2019). *The Danger Private Voucher School Programs Pose to Civil Rights.* (Report). Washington, DC: Center for American Progress.

Figlio, D., and C. Hart (2010). Competitive Effects of Means-Tested School Vouchers. *Working Paper16056.* Cambridge, MA: National Bureau of Economic Research. Retrieved from http://www/nber.org/papers/w16056.

Finn, Jr., C. E., C. Hentges, M. J. Petrilli, and A. Winkler (2009). *When Private Schools Take Public Dollars: What's the Place of Accountability in School Voucher Programs?* Washington, DC: Thomas B. Fordham Institute.

Fischer, B. (2013, January 3). ALEC's Schoolhouse Rock. *The Progressive.* Retrieved from www.progressive.org.

Fisher, D., and N. Frey (2021). *Better Learning through Structured Teaching: A Framework for the Gradual Release of Responsibility.* Alexandria, VA: Association for Supervision and Curriculum Development.

Fleming, D. J., J. M. Cowen, J. F. Witte, and P. J. Wolf (2013). Similar Students, Different Choices: Who Uses a School Voucher in an Otherwise Similar Population of Students? *Education and Urban Society (47)*7, 1–28. doi:10.1177/0013124513511268.

Ford, M. R. (2016, Winter). Funding Impermanence: Quantifying the Public Funds Sent to Closed Schools in the Nation's First Urban School Voucher Program. *Public Administration Quarterly (40)*4, 882–912.

Friedman, M. (1955). The Role of Government in Education. In Robert A. Solo (ed.), *Economics and the Public Interest,* 123–44. New Brunswick, NJ: Rutgers University Press. Retrieved from https://miltonfriedman.hoover.org/objects /58044//the-role-of-government-in-education.

Frost, R. (1942). *Collected Poems of Robert Frost.* Garden City, NY: Halcyon House.

Furman, G. (2012). Social Justice Leadership as Praxis: Developing Capacities through Preparation Programs. *Educational Administration Quarterly (48)*2. 191–229. Retrieved from https://eric.ed.gov/?id=EJ957152.

Gallo, Jr., P. J. (2014). Reforming the "Business" of Charter Schools in Pennsylvania. *B.Y.U. Education and Law Review (2014)*2, 206–32. Retrieved from: https:// digitalcommons.law.byu/elj/vol2014/iss2/3.

Garza, R. E., E. Garza Jr. (2010). Successful White Female Teachers of Mexican American Students of Low Socioeconomic Status. *Journal of Latinos and Education (9)*3, 189–206. doi:10.1080/15348431003761174.

Gilblom, E. A., and H. I. Sang (2019). Closure and the Roles of Student Performance and Enrollment Characteristics: A Survival Analysis of Charter Schools in Ohio's Largest Urban Counties. *Educational Policy Analysis Archives (27)*107, 1–36. Retrieved from https://doi.org/10.14507/epaa.27.4568.

Giroux, H. A. (2014). When Schools Become Dead Zones of the Imagination: A Critical Pedagogy Manifesto. *Policy Futures in Education (12)*4, 491–99. https:// doi.org.10.2304/pfie.2014.12.4.491.

Goldring, E., and W. Greenfield (2002). Understanding the Evolving Concept of Leadership in Education: Expectations, and Dilemmas. In J. Murphy (ed.), *The Educational Leadership Challenge: Redefining Leadership for the 21st Century,* 1–19. Chicago, IL: University of Chicago Press.

Goldstein, D. (2015). *The Teacher Wars: A History of America's Most Embattled Profession.* New York: Anchor Books.

Goldstein, D. (2017, April 11). Special Ed School Vouchers May Come With Hidden Costs. *New York Times.* Retrieved from https://myti.ms/2onz9kO.

Goleman, D., R. Boyatzis, and A. McKee (2004). *Primal Leadership: Learning to Lead with Emotional Intelligence.* Cambridge, MA: Harvard Business School Press.

Goodlad, J. (1990). *A Place Called School: Prospects for the Future.* New York: McGraw-Hill.

Gorman, N. (2016, December 6). Betsy DeVos: 9 Facts that Sum Up Everything You Need to Know. *Education World.* Retrieved from www.educationworld.com /a_news/betsy-devos-9-facts-sum-everything-you-need-know-1764143159.

Granger, D. A. (2008). No Child Left Behind and the Spectacle of Failing Schools: The Mythology of Contemporary School Reform. *Educational Studies 43,* 206–28. Doi:10.108000131940802117654.

Grose, J. (2022). "Who's Unhappy With Schools? The Answer Surprised Me." *New York Times, March 19, 2022,* Retrieved from https://www.nytimes.com/2022/03/19 /opinion/parents-schools.

Gunzenhauser, M. G., and A. M. Hyde (2007). What Is the Value of Public School Accountability? *Educational Theory, (57)*4, 489–507.

Gutmann, A., and S. Ben-Porah (2015). *Democratic Education.* In Michael T. Gibbons (ed.), *The Encyclopedia of Political Thought,* 1–12. West Sussex, UK: John Wiley & Sons, Ltd.

Hackett, U. (2017). Theorizing the Submerged State: The Politics of Private Schools in the United States. *The Policy Studies Journal (45)*3, 464–89. doi:10.1111/ psj12170.

Hallinger, P. (2005). Instructional Leadership and the School Principal: A Passing Fancy that Refuses to Fade Away. *Leadership and Policy in Schools* 4(1), 1–20. doi:10.108015700760500244793.

Hampton, F. M. (2016). The Seven Secrets of Successful Urban School Students: The Evidence Continues to Grow. *Education and Urban Society (48)*5, 423–43. doi:10.1177/00131124514533990.

Hanushek, E. A. (2020). The Unavoidable: Tomorrow's Teacher Compensation. (Policy Analysis). Stanford, CA: The Hoover Institute.

Hartman, D. A. (2005). Constitutional Responsibility to Provide a System of Free Public Schools: How Relevant Is the States' Experience to Shaping Governmental Obligations in Emerging Democracies? *Syracuse Journal of International Law and Commerce* 33:95, 95–114.

Hefling, K. (2017, October 30). How the Kochs Are Trying to Shake Up Public Schools., One State at a Time. *Politico.* Retrieved from https://www.politico.com/ story/2017/10/30/kochs-public-schools-shakeup-244259?cmpid=sf.

Herron, A. (2022a, January 2). "Bills to Ban Some Concepts at Schools Filed" *Indianapolis Star, January 2, 2022,* p. 23A.

Herron, A. (2022b, February 20). "'It's the Last Nail in the Coffin.'" *Indianapolis Star, February 20, 2022,* p. 1A, p. 8A-10A.

Hess, F. M. (2010). Does School Choice "Work"? *National Affairs,* Fall, 35–53. Retrieved from www.nationalaffairs.com/publications/detail/does-school-choice -work.

Hicks, M. (2022). School Choice and Student Transfers. *The Country Economist.* Retrieved from www.michaeljhicks.substack.com.

Hopkins, D. (2003). Instructional Leadership and School Improvement. In Alma Harris et al. (eds.), *Effective Leadership for School Improvement,* 112–35. London: RoutledgeFalmer.

Hostetler, K. (2003). The Common Good and Public Education. Book Review. In *Educational Theory, (53)*3, 347–61. doi.10.1111/j.1741-5446.2003.00347.

Hunter, M. (1982). *Mastery Teaching.* Thousand Oaks, CA: Corwin Press.

Hursh, D. (2007). Assessing No Child Left Behind and the Rise of Neoliberal Education Policies. *American Educational Research Journal (44)*3, 493–518.

Ignelzi, M. (2000). Meaning-making in the Learning and Teaching Process. *New Directions for Teaching and Learning 82,* 5–14. Retrieved from https://doi.org/10.1002/tl.8201.

Ilgen, D. R., J. R. Hollenbeck, M. Johnson, and D. Jundt (2005). Teams in Organizations: From Input-Process-Output Models to IMOI Models. *Annual Review of Psychology 56,* 517–43. doi:10.1146/annurev.psych.56.091103.070250.

Imoukhuede, A. A. (2019). Enforcing the Right to Public Education. *Arkansas Law Review 72:2,* 443–65.

Ingersoll, R. M., and G. J. Collins (2017). Accountability and Control in American Schools. *Journal of Curriculum Studies* 49(1), 75–95. doi:10.1080/00220272.2016.1205142.

Jackson, C. K., R. C. Johnson, and C. Persico, C. (2016). The Effects of School Spending on Educational and Economic Outcomes: Evidence from School Finance Reforms. *The Quarterly Journal of Economics*, 157–218. doi:10.1093/qje/qjv036.

Jensen, J. L., M. A. McDaniel, S. M. Woodard, and T. A. Kummer (2014). Teaching to the Test . . . or Testing to Teach: Exams Requiring Higher Order Thinking Skills Encourage Greater Conceptual Understanding. *Educational Psychology Review 26,* 307–29. doi:10.1007/s10648-013-9248-9.

Kaufman, B. C. (2017, February 13). School Vouchers Bring More Money to Catholic Schools—but at a Cost, Study Finds. *Notre Dame News.* Retrieved from http://news.ndd.edu/news/school-vouchers-bring-more-money-to-catholic-schools-but-at-a-cost-study-finds.

Kegan, R. (1980). Making Meaning: The Constructive-Developmental Approach to Persons and Practice. *The Personnel and Guidance Journal,* 373–80. doi:10.1002/j21644918.1980.tb00416.

Klein, R. (2017, December 26). Voucher Schools Championed by Betsy DeVos Can Teach Whatever They Want. Turns Out They Teach Lies. *HuffPost.* Retrieved from https://www.huffingtonpost.com/entry/school-voucher-evangelical.

Knight Abowitz, K. (2008). On the Public and Civic Purposes of Education. (Book Review) *Educational Theory (58)*3, 357–76.

Knight Abowitz, K. (2018). The War on Public Education: Agonist Democracy and the Fight for Schools as Public Things. *Philosophical Inquiry in Education* 25(1), 1–15.

Knight Abowitz, K. and S. M. Stitzlein (2018). Public Schools, Public Goods, and Public Work. *Kappan* 100(3), 33–37.

Kohlberg, L., and R. H. Hersh (1977). Moral Development: A Review of the Theory. *Theory into Practice (16)*2, 53–59. Retrieved from http://links.jstor.org/sici=00405841%28197704%2916%3A2%3C53%3AMDAROT%3E2.0.CO%3B2-%23.

Krathwohl, D. R. (2002). A Revision of Bloom's Taxonomy: An Overview. *Theory Into Practice (41)*4, 212–18. Retrieved from https://www.depauw.edu/files/resources/krathwohl.

Kurth-Schai, R. (2014). Fidelity in Public Education Policy: Reclaiming the Deweyan Dream. *Educational Studies 50,* 420–46. doi:10.1080/00131946.2014.943892.

Labby, S., F. C. Lunenburg, and J. R. Slate (2012). Emotional Intelligence and Academic Success: A Conceptual Analysis for Educational Leaders. *International Journal of Educational Leadership Preparation* 7(1), 1–11.

Laguardia, A., and A. Pearl (2009). Necessary Educational Reform for the 21st Century: The Future of Public Schools in Our Democracy. *The Urban Review.* 41(4), 352–68.

Lapsley, D. K. (2008). Moral Self-Identity and the Aim of Education. In Larry P. Nucci and Darcia Narvaez (eds.), *Handbook of Moral and Character Education,* 30–50. New York: Routledge.

Lee, J. (2018). Understanding Site Selection of For-Profit Educational Management Organization Charter Schools. *Education Policy Analysis Archives (26)*77, 3–17. Retrieved from http://dx.doi.org/10/14507/epaa.26.3024.

Leo, U., and P. Wickenberg (2013). Professional Norms in School Leadership: Change Efforts in Implementation of Education for Sustainable Development. *Journal of Educational Change, 14,* 403–22. doi:10.1007/s10833-013-9207-8.

Levin, H. M. (2002). A Comprehensive Framework for Evaluating Educational Vouchers. *Educational Evaluation and Policy Analysis, (24)*3, 159–74. Retrieved from https://www.jstor.org/stable/3594163.

Lewis, J. (2012). *Across that bridge: Life lessons and a vision for change.* New York: Legacy Lit.

Loeb, S., J. Valant, and M. Kasman (2011). Increasing Choice in the Market for Schools: Recent Reforms and their Effects on Student Achievement. *National Tax Journal, (64)*1, 141–64. Retrieved from https://cepa.stanford.edu/sides/default/files/A06-Loeb.pdf.

Logan, J. R., and J. Burdick-Will (2015). School Segregation, Charter Schools, and Access to Quality Education. *Journal of Urban Affairs (38)*3, 323–43. doi:10.1111/juaf.12246.

Lubienski, C. (2013). Privatising Form or Function? Equity, Outcomes and Influence in American Charter Schools. *Oxford Review of Education, (39)*4, 398–513. Retrieved from http://dx.doi.org/10.1080/03054985.2013.821853.

Lubienski, C., C. Gulosino, and P. Weitzel (2009). School Choice and Competitive Incentives: Mapping the Distribution of Educational Opportunities across Local Education Markets. *American Journal of Education, 115,* 601–47. Retrieved from http://www.jstor.org/stable/10.1086/599778.

Ludwig, J. (2022, April 23). "Opinion: The Surprising Solution to Gun Violence." CNN, April 23, 2022. Retrieved from https://www.cnn.com.

Mann, H. (1839). *Report for 1839.* Annual Reports of the Secretary of the Board of Education. Retrieved from https://archive.org/details/annualreportsse00manngoog.

Matusov, E., K. von Duyke, and S. Kayumova, S. (2016). Mapping Concepts of Agency in Educational Contexts. *Integrative Psychology and Behavioral Science* 50, 420–46. doi:10:1007/s12124-015-9336-0.

McFarland, J., B. Hussar, J. Zhang, X. Wang, K. Wang, S. Hein, . . . A. Barmer (2019). *The Condition of Education 2019 (NCES 2019–144).* U.S. Department of Education. Washington, DC: National Center for Education Statistics. Retrieved from https://nces.ed.gov/pubsearch/pubsinfo.asp?pubid=2019144.

McKinley, W., S. Latham, and M. Braun, M. (2014). Organizational Decline and Innovation: Turnarounds and Downward Spirals. *Academy of Management Review* 39(1), 88–110.

McWilliam, E. (2008). Unlearning How to Teach. *Innovations in Education and Teaching International (45)*3, 263–69. Doi:10.1080/1470322908022176147.

Mead, R. (2016, December 14). Betsy DeVos and the Plan to Break Public Schools. "Daily Comment," *New Yorker.* Retrieved from www.newyorker.com/news/daily -comment/betsy-devos-and-the-plan-to-break-public-schools.

Mercer, N. (2013). The Social Brain, Language, and Goal-Directed Collective Thinking: A Social Conception of Cognition and Its Implications for Understanding How We Think, Teach, and Learn. *Educational Psychologist (48)*3, 148–68. Retrieved from https://doi.org/10.1080/004611520.2013.804394.

Merritt, C. C., S. S. Kennedy, and M. D. Farnworth, M. D. (2020). The Civic Dimension of School Voucher Programs. *Public Integrity* 22(2), 154–69.

Miller, P., M. Scanlan, and N. Wills (2014). Leadership on the Social Frontier: The Role of the Principal in Comprehensive Reform Settings. *Principal's Research Review* (9)2, 1–6. Reston, VA: National Association of Secondary School Principals.

Molden, D. C., and E. T. Higgins (2012). Motivated Thinking. In Kenneth J. Holyoak and Robert G. Morrison, (eds.), *The Oxford Handbook of Thinking and Reasoning,* 390–412. Oxford, UK: Oxford University Press.

Molloy, M. C. (2022). "Mom Has Plan to Stamp out CRT" *Indianapolis Star,* February 20, 2022, p. 1A, 5A.

Molnar, A., G. Miron, N. Elgeberi, M. K. Barbour, L. Huerta, S. R.Shafer, and J. K. Rice (2019). *Virtual Schools in the U.S. 2019.* Boulder, CO: National Education Policy Center. Retrieved from http://nepc.colorado.edu/publication/virtual-schools -annual-2019.

Moon, J. S., and M. S. Stewar (2016, October). Understanding How School Vouchers Are Funded: Summary of Funding for the Indiana Choice Scholarship Program. Research Brief: Center for Evaluation & Education Policy (CEEP). Bloomington, IN: Indiana University School of Education.

Moyers, B. (2014). *Understanding the Propaganda Campaign Against Public Education.* Perspectives Blog. Retrieved from http://billmoyers.com/2014/03/25.

Murphy, J., C. M. Neumerski, E. Goldring, J. Grissom, and A. Porter (2016). Bottling Fog? The Quest for Instructional Management. *Cambridge Journal of Education* 46(4), 255–471. doi:10.1080/0305764X.2015.1064096.

Murray, K., and K. R. Howe, K. R. (2017). Neglecting Democracy in Educational Policy: A-F School Report Card Accountability Systems. *Educational Policy Analysis Archives* 25(109), 2–22. doi:10.14507/epaa.25.3017.

National Center for Education Statistics (NCES). (2022). *Fast Facts: Expenditures.* Retrieved from www.nces.ed.gov.

National Commission on Excellence in Education. (1983). *A Nation at Risk: The Imperative for Educational Reform.* Washington, DC: United States Department of Education.

Northouse, P. G. (2007). Culture and Leadership. In Peter G. Northouse (ed.), *Leadership: Theory and Practice,* 335–76. Thousand Oaks, CA: Sage Publications.

Nucci, L. P. (2008). Social Cognitive Domain Theory and Moral Education. In Larry P. Nucci and Darcia Narvaez (eds.), *Handbook of Moral and Character Education,* 291–309. New York: Routledge.

Nutt, P. C. (2004). Organizational De-development. *Journal of Management Studies (41)7,* 1083–1103.

Otremba, E. (2020). History of the Future: A Powerful Way to Teach the Past (and Present). *History Teacher (53)4,* 707–31.

Partelow, L., S. Shapiro, A. McDaniels, and C. Brown (2018, September 20). *Fixing Chronic Disinvestment in K-12 Schools.* Washington, DC: Center for American Progress.

Penn State Sites. (2019). *The Price of Standardized Testing—Education.* Retrieved from https://sites.psu.edu/total9edu/2019/02/07/the-price-of-standardized-testing/.

Perkins, D., and S. Tishman (2016). Patterns of Thinking: An Investigation into the Nature of Critical and Creative Thinking. *Project Zero Overview.* Cambridge, MA: Harvard Graduate School of Education.

Petrilli, M., C. Finn, C. Hentges, and A. M. Northern (2009). "When Private Schools Take Public Dollars: What's the Place of Accountability in School Voucher Programs?" Washington, DC: The Fordham Foundation. Retrieved from https://edexcellence.net/publications/when-private-schools-take.html.

Piaget, J. (1952). *The Origins of Intelligence in Children.* New York: International Universities Press.

Powell, M. (2021). In Texas, A Battle Over What Can Be Taught, and What Books Can Be Read. *New York Times,* December 10, 2021. Retrieved from https://www.nytimes.com.

Reckhow, S., M. Grossman, and B. C. Evans, B. C. (2015). Policy Cures and Ideology in Attitudes toward Charter Schools. *Policy Studies Journal (43)2.* Retrieved from https://doi.org/10.1111/psj.12093.

Rector-Aranda, A. (2016). School Norms and Reforms, Critical Race Theory, and the Fairytale of Equitable Education. *Critical Questions in Education (7)1,* 1–16.

Reimers, F. (2006). Citizenship, Identity, and Education: Examining the Public Purposes of Schools in an Age of Globalization. *Prospects, (36)3,* 275–94.

Rentner, D. S. (2019). Are Public School Teachers Adequately Compensated? (Report). Washington, DC: Center on Education Policy.

Rich, M. (2014, April 25). A Walmart Fortune, Spreading Charter Schools. *New York Times.* Retrieved from http://nyti.ms/1ldQYu5.

Ringold, D. J. (2005). Vulnerability in the Marketplace: Concepts, Caveats, and Possible Solutions. *Journal of Macromarketing, (25)2,* 202–14. doi:10.1177/0276146705281094.

Ritchart, R., and D. N. Perkins (2005). Learning to Think: The Challenges of Teaching Thinking. In Keith J. Holyoak and Robert G. Morrison (eds.), *The Cambridge Handbook of Thinking and Reasoning,* 775–802. Retrieved from https://pdfs.semanticscholar.org/0e3b/9e4de493894a79f579155c09f006ac88.

Rogers, R. (2015). Making Public Policy: The New Philanthropists and American Education. *American Journal of Economics and Sociology* 74(4), 743–74.

Rouse, C. E., and L. Barrow (2008, August 6). School Vouchers and Student Achievement: Recent Evidence, Remaining Questions. *Annual Review of Economics (1)*1. Retrieved from http://www.annualreviews.org.

Sass, T. R., R. W. Zimmer, B. P. Gill, and T. K. Booker (2016). Charter High Schools' Effects on Long-Term Attainment and Earnings. *Journal of Policy Analysis and Management (35)*3, 683–706. doi:10.1002/pam.21913.

Schmoker, M. J. (2006). *Results Now.* Arlington, VA: Association for Supervision and Curriculum Development.

Sciarra, D. G., and M. A. Hunter (2015). Resource Accountability: Enforcing State Responsibilities for Sufficient and Equitable Resources Used Effectively to Provide All Students a Quality Education. *Education Policy Analysis Archives (23)*21, n21.

Shaffer, M. B., and B. Dincher (2020). In Indiana, School Choice Means Segregation. *Kappan (101)*5, 40–43. https://doi.org/10.1177/0031721720903827.

Shaw, J. S. (2010). Education—A Bad Public Good? *The Independent Review (15)*2, 241–56.

Silverstein, J. (2021, November 12). The 1619 Project and the Long Battle Over U.S. History. *Pulitzer Center Update.* Washington, DC: Pulitzer Center. Retrieved from www.1619education.org.

Skinner, R. R. (2019, July 23). *State and Local Financing of Public Schools.* Washington, DC: Congressional Research Service.

Smith, V. (2017, January 22). Vic's Statehouse Notes #270. Retrieved from http://www.icpe-monroecounty.org/blog/vics-statehouse-otes-270-january-22-2017.

Spillane, J. P., L. M. Parise, and J. Zoltners Sherer (2011). Organizational Routines as Coupling Mechanisms: Policy, School Administration, and the Technical Core. *American Educational Research Journal* (48)3, 586–619. doi:10.3102/0002831210385102.

Stefkovich, J., and P. T. Begley (2007). Ethical School Leadership: Defining the Best Interests of Students. *Educational Management Administration & Leadership* 35(2), 205–24. doi:10.1177/1741143207075389.

Stein, M. L. (2015). Public School Choice and Racial Sorting: An Examination of Charter Schools in Indianapolis. *American Journal of Education 121,* 597–622.

Sternberg, R. J., and E. L. Grigorenko (2004). Successful Intelligence in the Classroom. *Theory Into Practice, (43)*4, 274–80. Retrieved from www.tandfonline.com/doi/abs/10.1207/s15430421tip4304_5.

Sternberg, R. J., A. Reznitskaya, and L. Jarvin (2007). Teaching for Wisdom: What Matters Is Not Just What Students Know, but How They Use It. *London Review of Education (5)*2, 143–58. doi:10.1080/14748460701440830.

Stitzlein, S. M. (2015). Addressing Educational Accountability and Political Legitimacy with Citizen Responsibility. *Educational Theory (65)*5, 563–80.

Stitzlein, S. M. (2017, September 5). How to Define Public Schooling in the Age of Choice? *Education Week.* Retrieved from http://www.edweek.org/ew/articles/2017/09/06/how-to-define-public-schooling-in-the.html.

Strauss, V. (2016, December 14). The Reason America's Schools Are So Segregated and the Only Way to Fix It. *Washington Post.* December 14, 2016.

Strike, K. A. (2008). School, Community and Moral Education. In Larry P. Nucci and Darcia Narvaez (eds.), *Handbook of Moral and Character Education,* 117–33. New York: Routledge.

Suitts, S. (2016, November). Students Facing Poverty: The New Majority. *Educational Leadership (74)*3, 36–40.

Suitts, S. (2019, June 4). Segregationists, Libertarians, and the Modern "School Choice" Movement. Monograph. *Southern Spaces.* Retrieved from www .southernspaces.org.

Sullivan, L. H. (1896). The Tall Office Building Artistically Considered. *Lippincotts Magazine.*

Swensson, J., J. Ellis, and M. Shaffer (2019a). *Unraveling Reform Rhetoric: What Educators Need to Know and Understand.* London: Rowman & Littlefield.

Swensson, J., J. Ellis and M. Shaffer (2019b). *An Educator's GPS: Fending Off the Free Market of Schooling for America's Students.* London: Rowman & Littlefield.

Swensson, J., and M. Shaffer (2020). *Defining the Good School: Educational Adequacy Requires More than Minimums.* London: Rowman & Littlefield.

Swensson, J., and L Lehman (2021). *Reliable School Leadership: What All Students Deserve.* London: Rowman & Littlefield.

Swensson, J., L. Lehman, and J. Ellis (2021). *The Thief in the Classroom: How School Funding Is Misdirected, Disconnected, and Ideologically Aligned.* London: Rowman & Littlefield.

Taba, H. (1962). *Curriculum Development: Theory and Practice.* New York: Harcourt, Brace, & World, Inc.

Tichnor-Wagner, A., C. Harrison, and L. Cohen-Vogel (2016). Cultures of Learning in Effective High Schools. *Educational Administration Quarterly (52)*4, 602–42. doi:10:11770013161X16644957.

Umpstead, R. R. (2007). Determining Adequacy: How Courts Are Redefining State Responsibility for Educational Finance, Goals, and Accountability. *B.Y.U. Education and Law Journal, (2007)*2. Retrieved from https://digitalcommons.law .byu.edu/elj/vol2007/iss2/5.

Underwood, J., and J. F. Mead (2012). A Smart ALEC Threatens Public Education. *Phi Delta Kappa International, (93)*6, 51–55. Retrieved from http://www.edweek .org/ew/articles/2012/03/01/kappan_underwood.html?cmp=eml-contshr-shr-desk.

Urban, W. J., J. L. Wagoner, and M. Gaither (2019). *American Education: A History.* New York: Routledge.

Weathers, E. S., and V. E. Sosina (2019). Separate Remains Unequal: Contemporary Segregation and Racial Disparities in School District Revenue. (CEPA Working Paper No. 1902). Stanford, CA: Center for Education Policy Analysis. Retrieved from http://cepa.standford.edu/wp19-02.

Weaver, H. L. (2018, January 30). What Donald Trump, Mike Pence, and Betsy DeVos Won't Tell You About "School Choice." *Speak Freely.* Washington, DC: ACLU. Retrieved from https://www.aclu.org/blog/religious-liberty/religion-and -public-schools/what-donald-trump-mike-pence-and-betsy-devos-wont.

Webster, R. S. (2017). Valuing and Desiring Purposes of Education to Transcend Miseducative Measurement Practices. *Educational Philosophy and Theory* 49(4), 331–46. Retrieved from http://dx.doi.org/10.1080/00131857.2015.1052355.

Weitzel, W., and E. Jonsson (1989, March 1). Decline in Organizations: A Literature Integration and Extension. *Administrative Science Quarterly,* 91–109.

Westheimer, J., and J. Kahne (2003). Reconnecting Education to Democracy: Democratic Dialogues. *Phi Delta Kappan (85)*1, 9–14. Retrieved from https://eric .ed.gov/?id=EJ674581.

Whetten, D. A. (1980). Organizational decline: A neglected topic in organizational science. *Academy of Management review* 5(4), 577–88.

Wielkiewicz, R. M., and S. P. Stelzner (2005). An Ecological Perspective on Leadership Theory, Research, and Practice. *Review of General Psychology* 9(4), 66–85. doi:10.1037/1089-2680.9.4.326.

Wolf, P. J., A. Cheng, M. Batdorff, L. Maloney, J. F. May, and S. T. Speakman (2014). The Productivity of Public Charter Schools. (School Choice Demonstration Project). Fayetteville: University of Arkansas. Retrieved from www.uaedreform .org/the-productivity-of-charter-schools.

Wolfe, P. (2001). *Brain Matters: Translating Research into Classroom Practice.* Alexandria, VA: Association for Supervision and Curriculum Development.

Wong, K. K., and F. X. Shen (2006). Charter Law and Charter Outcomes: Re-Examining the Charter School Marketplace. Prepared for the National Conference on Charter School Research at Vanderbilt University, September 29, 2006. National Center on School Choice. Retrieved from https://eric.ed.gov/?id =ED509549.

Worrell, F. C. (2014). Theories School Psychologists Should Know: Culture and Academic Achievement. *Psychology in the Schools (51)*4, 332–47. doi:10.1002/ pits.21756.

Zernike, K. (2016, December 12). How Trump's Education Nominee Bent Detroit to Her Will on Charter Schools. *New York Times.* Retrieved from http://nyti.ms /2gzJXds.

Index

About the Author

Jeff Swensson, PhD, served for forty-five years in K-12 public education throughout the Midwest. His insights about the value of traditional public education are the result of service as a teacher, assistant principal, principal, associate superintendent, and superintendent in urban and suburban school districts. Swensson is the coauthor of five books. His dedication to student-centric teaching and learning reflects the essential relationship between US democracy and traditional public education.